What does she *want* from me,? anyway?

Holly Faith Phillips is available for a limited
number of speaking engagements.
For details, call Susan Yates.
(714) 285-9540

Honest Answers to the Questions
Men Ask About Women

What does she want from me, anyway?

Holly Faith Phillips

WITH GREGG LEWIS

ZondervanPublishingHouse
Grand Rapids, Michigan
HarperCollins*Publishers*
New York, New York

What Does She Want from Me, Anyway?
Copyright © 1997 by Holly Faith Phillips

Request for information should be addressed to:

Zondervan Publishing House
Grand Rapids, Michigan 49530

Library of Congress Cataloging-in-Publication Data

Phillips, Holly Faith.
What does she want from me, anyway? : honest answers to the questions men ask
about women / Holly Faith Phillips, with Gregg Lewis.
    p.   cm.
    ISBN: 0-310-21457-2
    1. Sex role. 2. Man-woman relationships. 3. Married people—Psychology. 4.
Interpersonal communication. 5. Intimacy (Psychology) I. Lewis, Gregg A. II. Title.
HQ1075.P48   1997
306.7—dc 21   97–1889
                                                                                  CIP

International Trade Paper Edition 0-310-21659-1

This edition is printed on acid-free paper and meets the American National Standards
Institute Z39.48 standard.

*Some names and identifying details have been changed to protect the privacy of people who
have shared their stories with the author.*

Scripture quotations, unless otherwise noted, are from *The Holy Bible, New International
Version* (NIV) © 1973, 1984 by International Bible Society, used by permission of
Zondervan Publishing House.

Published in association with Sealy M. Yates, Literary Agent, Orange, CA.

Interior design by Sue Vandenberg Koppenol

Printed in the United States of America

---

97 98 99 00 01 02 03 04 /❖ DH/ 10 9 8 7 6 5 4 3 2 1

To all the guys who care, who haven't quit,
and who are willing to go the distance ...

Contents

Part One
CAN YOU PLEASE HELP ME UNDERSTAND?

Part Two
WHAT CAN I DO TO WIN HER BACK?

Acknowledgments

Grateful thanks to . . .

Randy for being to me the most dear, patient, and humble man of strength a woman could ask for. As a leader you have been my outstanding mentor, for I know none who is more gracious and wholeheartedly committed to Jesus Christ than you. Thank you for the best years of my life!

Our children, Timothy, Christian, and Kimberly. You mean more to me than any ministry or personal aspiration. You are to be applauded for your incredible capacity for love, forgiveness, adaptation, and support. We are so grateful God gave us you three to enrich our lives so deeply.

Our home group (Dale and Liz, James and Belinda, Gary and Carrie, Bill and Lyndi) for your faithfulness, your forbearance, and always being there for us when we need you. (This includes you too, Gary Smalley!) Through you, I have learned to love and trust others again. Thank you for helping remove the grave clothes and for bringing me out into the sunlight. Thank you too for the crucial input on the editing process. I love you so much. Isaiah 60.

Stan Endicott and the Promise Band Teams; Tom and Maria Vegh; Buddy and Linda Owens; Chuck and Stess Fromm; and Malcolm Duplessis. You were used to help "restore the years the locusts had eaten." What an extended family you turned out to be. I can't imagine life without you. I love you!

Doug Feil—the ray of sunshine in the midst of our storm, born for such a time as this. Randy and I owe you a world of gratitude.

Bob and Karen Foster and all the Lost Valley Ranch staff. We did it! Thanks for being so accommodating and for cheering us on. OOOAH!

Pete and Janet Richardson for being faithful friends and for bringing spice and youthful adventure into our lives to keep us from growing old before our time.

Sealy Yates, for the wise and gentle way you shepherded me through the process. This book would not have been without your agenting savvy, your tender heart, or your sensitive Christian spirit.

All my publishing friends at Zondervan/HarperCollins. I not only appreciate your editorial skills and judgments, but your belief in me and your vision for this book.

Gregg Lewis. I have been privileged to work with you. Thank you for all your wisdom, male perspective, expertise, and friendship. Zondervan was right!

Mom ... you're the best! I love you!

And to Jesus. Thank you for everything. For never giving up on me, nor giving in to me, for holding your ground and remaining unshakable in your love. You are the dearest to my heart, and without you, life would be void of meaning.

Words from the Coach

As a former collegiate football player for the Missouri Tigers, I testify from painful experience when I say there are few things that happen on a football field which can shake a linebacker's confidence more than a blind-side hit. Once the ball is snapped, everything happens in a flash. As the quarterback pivots to hand off to the tailback, your primary responsibility becomes clear; you are to make sure that ballcarrier does not cross your side of the line of scrimmage.

Correctly anticipating the play you know is about to unfold, you race to fill the gap where the halfback thinks he will find running room. You're moving at full speed, with nothing between you and your target, a split second from making a tremendous tackle, when out of nowhere, like a stealth buffalo, some 290-pound offensive lineman plants his shoulder pad in your rib cage and launches you out of the play on an unexpected flight that ends in a bone-jarring crash landing about the same time the ballcarrier slashes into your secondary on his way to a game-breaking run.

The horrible jumble of feelings a linebacker gets when that happens reminds me of something that happened to me a couple years ago on a beautiful fall Sunday morning. I was not on a football field, but in the seemingly safe surroundings of my home church. The blind-side hit I was about to receive was not going to be from some oversized earthly opponent, but from the Spirit of Almighty God.

I felt a heightened sense of anticipation as the congregational singing ended and the guest speaker was introduced. The previous Sunday my pastor had announced we would be hearing this day from a gentleman who had spoken around the globe—a man who was going to address one of the most important truths he had learned in over fifty years of ministry.

The speaker began his sermon by combining gentle humor and some general background on his topic. But there was nothing in his words to warn me that he was about to make a statement that would alter the course of my life forever. Suddenly, out of nowhere, I heard him say: "If you want to measure the worth of a man's effectiveness in life, all you have to do is look on the countenance of his wife." These simple words from a humble servant, combined with the convicting penetration of the Spirit of God, rocked me to the core.

As I turned to look at my wife, Lyndi, what I saw was a woman whose eyes showed the sadness and pain of thirty-one years spent yielding to my personal pursuits and dreams—at her expense. As a college football coach I had sought and captured national championships while she had sought, but never captured, the full heart of her husband.

Hit hard by this sudden realization, I could only sit and weep. Soon thereafter I would resign my position as football coach at the University of Colorado, to finally learn, by the grace of God, what it meant to be a *real* man. I had been knocked off my lifelong course of selfish pursuits and sent sailing in an entirely different direction—to begin a new life of honoring and loving my faithful and precious wife.

Which brings me to the reason I accepted the invitation to open this book.

Lyndi and I probably know Holly Phillips and her husband, Randy, as well as we know any couple. We not only have served Promise Keepers together from the beginning, we've been covenant partners in a small group with three other couples who have met together regularly for more than four years now. We have shared hopes, pain, disappointment,

and growth. I have the greatest respect and love for them—
not just as friends or fellow laborers—but as transparent
models who (like Lyndi and I) have survived a devastating
avalanche of self-inflicted violations and mistakes in their
marriage to finally emerge as a strong, victorious couple who
are now experiencing the intended fullness of their marriage
relationship. Like all of us, they are very human. They have
hurt and been hurt. But they have also found healing and
hope, which Holly desperately wishes to share with you in
her own pointed and poignant way.

As you well know, we men respond best to simple,
basic guidelines. We always want to know what the rules
are and what part we're expected to play in the game. So if
you'll permit me, I'd like to use another football analogy
that might help you prepare to gain from Holly's insights.

Reading the first half of this book is going to seem a lot
like time spent in the film room where we watch and study
old film clips of previous games in preparation for the
upcoming season. What are we watching for? Our weaknesses and mistakes which make us most vulnerable. This
can be a painful, discouraging, and wearisome process. But
these are clips we can learn from. And the intent is that we
will benefit from reviewing our past failings.

However, it's easy to get discouraged when you look
back and focus only on past performances and last season's
dismal record. You can feel hopeless and lost before you
even begin—until you realize there are some basic, fundamental techniques you can master. Then you begin to
rediscover hope.

That is why the second half of this book could be
likened more to the practice field. Here is where we spell
out our game plan and rehearse the various pieces of our
strategy. Here is where we learn how to correct bad habits
and stupid mistakes and prepare to overcome both the
failings of our past and the adversity of the present to

become future champions. Here is where you will learn those simple, practical "techniques" that will restore your confidence and give you every reason to hope.

I expect many of you are thinking, "I know my weaknesses and mistakes. Just show me how to fix them." So you will be tempted to skip right past the first half of this book. Don't! You will be bypassing the process in order to get a quick solution—which has gotten many of us in the predicaments we are in today. As a coach, I would never allow my players to do that. NO PAIN, NO GAIN!

To get my attention God had to use a devastating blind-side jolt that shook me to my soul. For some guys he needs only a still, small voice to help turn their lives around and give them new direction. I expect he will use this book both ways. The words and stories that follow here will hit some of you so hard you'll feel like you're suddenly looking out the ear-hole of your helmets. Others of you may sense only a subtle nudge of the Holy Spirit. Be ready to respond to either possibility.

And as you begin to read, I'd like to challenge you with this reminder. The Champion of champions, Jesus Christ, was willing to endure the greatest of hardships for the sake of his Bride, the church. After you read these pages, may God grant you both the willingness and the strength to persevere and fulfill your calling to likewise be . . . a champion.

Bill McCartney,
Winter 1997

Preface

Before anything else is written here, I would like to say I'm impressed and personally encouraged that you care enough about your relationships to have picked up this book. That says a lot about you.

I suspect the very fact that I am a woman may have caused some of you men to approach this book with caution, because of the strain and threat continually being generated between men and women. But I hope you'll detect my heart and find value in the insights I share.

This is an age when men feel constantly challenged by women who refuse to be passive doormats any longer. And women sense they've been unappreciated and taken advantage of—whether it be on the home front or at the office. We've now gotten to the point where we need to understand each other. The era of declaring our rights and making sure that the other sex understands our complaints against them has met with few positive results. Something needs to change.

Rest assured, I do not perceive all the issues we men and women seem to be at odds over, as uniquely a male problem. I do not see men as the heavies in our marriages. I do see—in both camps—neglect, a serious lack of consideration, and outright dishonesty and immoral conduct that is deteriorating the fabric of many of our relationships. However, I will not arrogantly argue that men are the single cause. We women need to be honest and share the responsibility. We need to solve our problems together.

So let's imagine that I'm someone you already know very well. Maybe I'm a next-door neighbor. Or an old friend you grew up and went to school with. Or better yet, a sister who cares enough to listen carefully to your questions, understands you well enough to know the feelings behind your words, trusts you enough to sense your sincerity, and loves you enough to share whatever insights I've gained from my own experience.

I know that most experts, and even a few guys, are quick to conclude that "the males of our species simply don't know how to communicate. Men are verbally and emotionally challenged."

But I think those opinions unfairly sell men short. My own hopeful conclusion is this: We (you and I, men and women) can talk—honestly, openly, and productively. And that's just what we're going to do in the following pages.

In writing this book I feel as if I've run the first leg of a long relay race and am passing you the baton so that you can run the next leg. My job now is to watch you go and to cheer you on.

So don't be apprehensive about venturing forth. Be encouraged!

Holly Phillips,
Winter 1997

Who Is This Woman ...
And Why Is She Talking to Me?

During 1995, I had the unique privilege of talking face-to-face with three quarters of a million American men. This amazing opportunity came when I became the first woman invited to speak at the thirteen Promise Keepers conferences held in major sports arenas and stadiums around the country.

Each time I walked out on stage with the eyes of fifty, sixty, or seventy thousand men focused on me, my knees felt like jelly and a major butterfly migration started in my stomach. Yet on every occasion I felt my own natural nervousness and fear overcome by a supernatural sense of love and concern. Whenever I stood, a woman alone on the platform in the middle of a huge stadium filled with men, God gave me the ability to look out and up and around at the crowd and to see not one immense ocean of masculine humanity, but a collection of unique and separate faces. Row after row, section after section, of individuals. Ordinary guys. Brothers who were saying by their very presence at those events, *We want to be men of integrity. On the job. In our communities. And at home. We want to build meaningful relationships with God, with each other, and with women. We want to become more responsible men. More loving husbands. Better dads. We want to be everything we were created to be.*

What an incredible emotional experience for me as a woman! Standing on that platform, I was overwhelmed by the openness, the sincerity, the commitment, and the potential of all those men.

Many people who survive car accidents and other life-threatening ordeals talk about the phenomenon of having their lives flash before their eyes. In the same way, every time I stepped onto the stage, dozens of thoughts flashed through my mind in the moments before I began to speak.

What am I doing? Where do I start? What if they resent my being up here? Or simply misunderstand what I want to say? Where do I get off thinking I might speak on behalf of all the women today who might like to say something to their men? How will I know if these men are listening? How in the world did I get here anyway?

And yet, at the same time that wobbly-kneed, stomach-churning part of me was acknowledging all those doubts, my heart felt full-to-overflowing with some very different ideas.

I can do this. I want to do this. I need to do this. How do I convey the love and respect and concern I have for these guys? What can I say to encourage them in their individual quests to do and be better? What a terrific opportunity! What a remarkable responsibility! I can't imagine anything better than this incredible feeling of being here to support and encourage men. I'm having so much fun it almost feels illegal. Oh, God, this is absolutely awesome! Thank you!

Then I would begin to speak, suddenly confident in the realization that through God's mercy so much of my life experience, who I was, as well as what I've learned, had uniquely prepared me to stand on that stage.

MEN IN MY LIFE

I've always been comfortable with men.

I grew up as an Army brat with two brothers. We lived all over the world, on or around military bases where my father was stationed. From as early as I can remember, I've felt familiar with the masculine world.

A lot of men always hung around our house. My father's Army buddies came and went on a regular basis. So did my brothers' friends. At holiday time, Mom always invited at least a couple of homesick enlisted men to enjoy a traditional Thanksgiving or Christmas dinner with a real family.

In my teen years I cut my teeth as a performer singing for GIs at local service clubs. In the aftermath of Vietnam, I gained a very different perspective on men when I volunteered in a drug rehab and treatment center for war veterans.

I dated a number of guys before I met and married the man I've lived with for twenty-three years. Two of our three children are now teenage men. I've spent virtually all my adult professional life working very closely with men. Many, if not most, of my closest friends have been and are guys. So, at this point in life, I am well-acquainted with the male half of our species.

Not only is my husband, Randy, president of Promise Keepers, but I've worked since 1991 as one of the PK's earliest staff members. For almost two years I personally handled all the correspondence for Randy and the founder of Promise Keepers, Bill McCartney. I filled mail orders for products, managed the sales efforts at early conferences, and served as PK's official liaison to the music industry—helping spearhead the development and production of the first Promise Keeper music tapes. Until very recently, I oversaw the musical elements of all the conferences—assisting in planning and choosing the songs, finding and recruiting special music artists, and then monitoring and helping direct the musical segments of the program from backstage, from the production tent, or from a press box high in the stadium. So over the years

I've gotten some up close as well as bird's-eye perspectives on what began as the burning vision of a college football coach back in 1990 and has since exploded into a worldwide men's movement—touching the lives and families and communities of millions of men.

THE BAD AND THE UGLY

My many positive experiences with men have not only given me a very deep love and concern for men, but have made me comfortable talking to them.

However, I need to make it clear that by no means have all my interactions with men been positive. Indeed, some of the worst experiences I've had with men also have given me special motivation to reach out and speak at those conferences.

I don't love and respect and care about men because I've lived a sheltered life or a carefree existence under their benevolent protection. I'm neither inexperienced nor naive. I haven't been brainwashed because my husband happens to be an executive with an organization entrenched in the men's movement, and I'm not swayed by my loyalty to Randy.

In fact, nothing could be further from the truth.

I was molested as a young girl and experienced the shame of date rape in my teens. As an adult I spent years working in an environment with men who at times neither respected nor acknowledged my abilities, who so devalued me as a woman and a human being that I felt worse than worthless; I felt invisible. I was a nonperson taking up space.

But hardest and most painful of all were years four to fifteen of my marriage to Randy. I nearly lost myself in a relationship with a husband I felt didn't understand, support, affirm, value, truly love, or even care about me. I felt I had no place in my husband's heart. I'd lie awake at night and cry out to God: *Why am I here? Why am I alive? Why don't you let me die!* Despairing in the darkness beside my soundly sleeping husband I'd plead, *Lord, help me! Move this guy! Wake him up!*

I prayed that prayer for so many years, seemingly to no avail, that my heart gradually hardened to the point there was no feeling left. It was as if I'd flat-lined—like a heart monitor when the patient dies and no activity registers. When those prayers were ultimately answered and Randy did awaken to understand, support, affirm, value, love, and care about me, there was one problem. I could no longer respond. My heart had grown stone cold.

It took a *divine* degree of patient love and almost three years of counsel before the scars on my wounded heart finally healed. Only then with God's help could we rebuild our marriage into the remarkably strong, vital, and life-giving relationship it has become for both of us today.

QUESTIONS MEN ASK

The sum total of all my life experience—the good, the bad, and the ugly—enabled me to stand up and speak in front of hundreds of thousands of men. My life had given me something I felt was important to communicate. For I have become convinced that "the God of all comfort," as the Bible so eloquently puts it, "comforts us in all our troubles, so that we can comfort those in any trouble with the comfort we ourselves have received from God" (2 Corinthians 1:3–4).

I'll describe what I said to comfort and encourage all those men at the conferences in later chapters. But this book isn't so much about what I said as it is about what I've heard and seen and experienced in these last years of working in such close proximity to men.

The response I've received in the aftermath of those conferences has been far more astonishing, and even more gratifying, than the opportunity to speak in the first place.

From the time I walked off the stage at that very first conference, men have sought me out. They've stood by the
edge of the stage at the end of conference sessions. They've
cornered me in crowded stadium corridors. They've
flagged me down in parking lots outside. I've also received
more than my share of letters.

Most of these men have stories they want to tell. Some
have confessions to make. Many have pain and frustration
they need to express. Others have hopes and dreams they
wish to share. They all have questions about the most
important relationships in their lives. And often they were
looking for a woman to provide answers to those questions.

This book has been inspired and shaped by those
heartfelt, sometimes gut-wrenching, questions men have
asked me:

What does she want from me, anyway?

How do I get her to respect me?

When she says I don't value her, what does she mean?

How long do I have to pay for my mistakes?

Whatever happened to the woman I married?

*What does she mean when she says, "It's always been
about you"?*

*What can I do or say to make her feel we're communi-
cating?*

Why does sex have to be such a touchy issue?

*Does there always have to be a power struggle? It feels
like a never-ending tug-of-war.*

*Why do I always get the distinct impression I'm the
cause of all our problems?*

What can I do to show her I really care?

Where do I start if I want to make things better?

How can I rekindle the spark and recapture her heart?

Do you see any hope? Or is it too late?

I've heard men ask these questions over and over
again. My own husband has sometimes asked these questions about me.

I don't claim to have all the answers. I'm not a professional counselor, and I'm not an expert on relationships. Much of the wisdom I have to share will be drawn from the hard lessons Randy and I have learned from our relationship, with the help of God, who is an important part of our lives. I'm also drawing from my own life experience, from observations and insights gained through my own interaction with men in Promise Keepers, and from the people who have asked questions, shared stories, and admitted struggles while looking for some kind of answer that would give hope.

BREAKING DOWN THE WALLS

In February 1996, Promise Keepers sponsored a special conference attended by more than 40,000 ministers from North America and around the globe in what may have been the largest single multidenominational assembly of Christian pastors in history. But what excited me most wasn't so much the significant size of the event as the challenge laid out for this great gathering of grassroots spiritual leaders. Speaker after speaker called on these pastors to begin to "Break Down the Walls" that exist in our local communities and throughout society—walls between a man and God, between a man and other men, between denominations, and especially between ethnic groups.

As I stood enjoying the inspiration of the messages I was hearing and basking in the spirit of that conference, best-selling author, conference speaker, and dear friend Gary Smalley walked up to me and said something I haven't been able to get out of my mind since. "You know, Holly," said Gary, "there's one group not represented here with whom we need to reconcile."

Looking out at the multiracial crowd I saw African-Americans, Native Americans, Asian-Americans, Hispanic-Americans, and Anglo-Americans. The audience was a beautiful tapestry of brotherhood. "Who do you mean?" I asked.

"Women," he said. "We as men need to be reconciled with women."

I couldn't believe a man would make such a declaration. Frankly, I was stunned. And I knew what Gary had just said was right.

A lot of towering walls separate, isolate, and alienate people in our world today. Some walls are spiritual. Others are psychological. Some barriers are social. Others are economic. Or racial. As an individual and as a Christian, since long before Promise Keepers even began, I've been committed to breaking down whatever walls confine and limit us as human beings. Of all the barriers that prevent people from enjoying and experiencing the abundance of life and realizing the full potential with which we were created, the most basic may be that age-old, yet very contemporary, division between the sexes.

A very real wall towers between men and women today. You can't actually see it—either up close or from outer space where astronauts can spot the Great Wall of China winding its way across the world's largest continent. Yet this wall between the sexes seems in some ways more extensive and formidable than that ancient Asian structure; it stretches around the world and divides all of humanity right down the middle by separating us into two distinct camps. No armed guards are stationed atop this barrier separating men and women; yet it may be more confining than any prison wall in the world. No diplomatic checkpoints, no internationally recognized territorial boundaries exist; yet it's probably a greater barrier to human freedom than the old Berlin Wall and all the barbed-wire borders of the old Iron Curtain combined.

Many of us have learned to cope with this reality. We live out our daily personal and professional existence in its shadow. Since "the wall" is invisible, we often try to ignore it. But it's always there. And we can never completely forget it because we bump up against it every day of our lives.

This wall restricted and defined my life for many years—limiting my accomplishments, crippling me spiritually and emotionally, thwarting my personal happiness, and nearly destroying my marriage and family. I've seen it wreak similar havoc in the lives of many women friends. I know it does the same thing in the relationships of many desperate men who have asked me for words of hope and counsel at Promise Keepers conferences. This divide is the underlying problem behind every question men ask me.

There *is* a huge, horrible wall between men and women. And that needs to come down. I'm convinced that if men and women are to achieve a higher goal in our relationships, we're going to have to do more than maneuver around the barriers that separate us. We're going to have to dismantle the walls systematically. We're going to have to do more than acknowledge and resign ourselves to our differences. We're going to have to use and build on those distinctions. We're going to have to do more than simply see, accept, and tolerate each other as alien creatures from different planets (whether Mars or Venus); we're going to have to come together and embrace each other as two pieces to the same human puzzle, or two halves of the same whole. This was God's plan for men and women and marriage from the beginning: "And the two shall become one" (Genesis 2:24).

But before that can happen, what Gary Smalley reminded me is true: Men and women are going to have to be reconciled.

How do we get there? Where do we start? With understanding. Every one of the questions I hear from men could be prefaced with the clause, "Please help me understand ..." Please help me understand, why is she so angry? Please help me understand, what does she mean when she says I don't value her? Please help me understand ...

part *1*

Can You Please Help Me Understand?

chapter 1

Why Is She So Angry?
Discovering What Fuels Her Fire

I will never ever forget a lunch Randy and I shared one spring day in 1990. I don't recall exactly what had prompted my foul mood on this occasion. I almost always seemed upset about something. Or nothing. Or everything. In fact, for years, my family had lived in the shadow of my volcanic anger. Like most volcanoes, my mountain of inner anger was dangerously unpredictable. I could (and often did) erupt without warning, spewing fiery words and venting feelings that sent my husband and children seeking emotional cover. I tried desperately to contain myself, to keep the emotional heat and intensity tightly battened down and covered up. But suppression only worked for a limited time while creating a pressure cooker inside me. The intensity would rise and build until the anger erupted again. As a clear and disturbing consequence of those explosions, all of us bore a variety of serious scars.

On this particular day, even though I had my anger deeply buried, my true feelings were obvious to Randy. Not because he felt the heat, but because he felt the chill. I greeted him when he walked in the door, and I set his plate in front of him the moment he sat down at the dining-room table, but my words, my actions, and my entire manner were so cold and callous that Randy found no comfort in my presence or in the meal I'd prepared. I don't know if the strained silence between us finally prompted his next words, or if he'd come home planning to say what he said. But eventually he met my icy gaze and said very hesitantly, "Holly, we can't go on like this. I think you need to consider getting some professional help."

At that moment as I looked across the table at my husband, everything in me wanted to plant my fist in his face. I still have no idea what I said, but I'll never forget how angry and insulted I felt, or what I was thinking. *I can't believe you can sit there calmly eating the lunch I prepared for you and say that. For five years I've been asking if we could get some counsel, some help. All this time you've been saying, "No, I'm sure we can work it out. We can get through this on our own." I've been begging for help for years, and now you can't take me anymore. You can't deal with my anger, so you're gonna suggest I get help? How dare you!*

Randy knew I was angry. I left no doubt about that. Yet he couldn't begin to understand why. And on a deeper level, neither did I.

AN HONEST QUERY

Many of you men reading this book face the same dilemma that Randy and I faced seven years ago. You are asking, or have at some point in your life asked, about some woman in your life: "Why is she so angry?" I've heard this question from enough concerned men to believe it's an honest query. So I'm going to attempt to address the question with thoughtfulness and candor both because the question deserves it and because I believe you genuinely desire a forthright response.

I'll warn you now that you may not like all the answers I will suggest. I know Randy and I certainly learned many things that pained us to accept. I also know that not every answer I have to share will ring true for your life and your relationships. But I'm confident many of them will. I trust you to honestly acknowledge and apply those which do.

I'm also certain if you keep reading long enough, you'll encounter some points and insights that will catch you by surprise. I'm hopeful you will eventually conclude that my answers prove as fair and respectful as you and your question deserve.

For whether we are male or female, I believe it requires a willing and tenacious honesty even to attempt to answer this question and the others being asked throughout this book. I find great hope in Jesus' promise: "Then you will know the truth, and the truth will set you free" (John 8:32). Randy and I have found that always to be the case in our lives; I pray it will prove the same for you.

FRUSTRATION, FEAR, AND PAIN

So, *why is she so angry?*

Like so many of the men who come to me to talk about the angry women in their lives, both Randy and I assumed *anger* was the basic problem. It wasn't.

Since anger is often so tangible and so destructive, it's easy to fixate on it. We view anger as the problem when it's almost always just a symptom of a deeper, more serious, underlying issue. As I discovered through years of wise counsel, intense anger is often grown from the seeds of frustration, fear, and pain. If you truly want to know why a woman is angry, you'll need to probe a little deeper into these three areas:

1. What is she frustrated about?
2. Is she afraid? What is she afraid of?
3. Has she been hurt? What pain is she coping with?

Many scenarios and situations can trigger frustration, fear, and pain. I'll look at three: frustration when expectations for marriage are not fulfilled; fear triggered by financial insecurity; and pain from abuse or marital infidelity.

FRUSTRATION: WHEN MARRIAGE DOESN'T LIVE UP TO OUR EXPECTATIONS

After women walk down the aisle, many of them subconsciously expect the men they have married to take up where their attentive and providing dads left off. Some women who come from unhealthy homes where their dads were abusive, were absent in spirit, or abandoned them altogether, are often hoping for a man who will be everything their father was not—adoring, attentive, dependable, and concerned about the things that matter most to them.

If we're really truthful, a lot of us women have to admit we still long for a prince on a white horse who will carry us off into the sunset to live happily ever after. Most women, however, will not own up to such a dream because it implies the need for a man. And that admission just isn't cool in our day and age.

No matter what our background—whether we grew up in a secure environment where all our needs were met and we want that pattern to continue, or we endured an unhappy family situation and now hope to be rescued and offered a better existence—most of us venture into romantic relationships with high hopes and expectations. If and when those expectations aren't met, the result can be fear, hurt, frustration—and ultimately anger.

By way of encouragement, let me say this. Don't be over-whelmed here, gentlemen. It's been unreasonable for us to expect you to become the sole source of our happiness, or to be an extension of our dads. It's especially unreasonable for us to expect you to exhibit in your youth the maturity of one who has walked the miles and survived the battles of those twice your age. We clearly need to cut you a little slack when it comes to our unrealistic expectations.

At the same time I hope you will come to realize that most of us have never thought through our unfair expectations or considered their implications for our feelings and our relationships. And I hope you will recognize some of the legitimate reasons our unfulfilled expectations have added to our anger. In particular, two unmet expectations seem to weigh heavily on the minds of most wives. They want a father to help with the responsibility of raising their children. And they want a coworker to share in the work of maintaining their home.

The Trials of Raising a Family

When most couples start their families, few of them fully grasp or have even seriously discussed all the responsibilities entailed in parenthood. That's not too surprising since I doubt anyone in the history of the world has ever been fully prepared to become a parent. The enormity of the job sinks in only after the responsibilities have arrived.

Yet the job stress that comes with raising a family can weigh especially heavy on any individual who has been told (or soon learns on her own) that she's expected to assume the duties of nurse, teacher, disciplinarian, chauffeur, coach, trainer, cheerleader, referee, chaplain, scheduling secretary, bookkeeper, chief operating officer, and janitor of a 24-hour-a-day, 7-day-a-week, 365-day-a-year operation that boasts a full-time, unpaid, and overwhelmed staff of one. And that's a fairly accurate job description in too many families today where women are forced into, or assume out of necessity, the dual roles of father and mother.

It should come as no great surprise that the resulting stress first produces intense frustration, then some rage. That conclusion was supported by the research done for this book. While poring over the letters women have sent to our Promise Keepers office, I discovered that the number-two need they expressed (number one will be addressed later on) was this: "I need help raising our family. My children need two parents. My kids would love so much for their dad to be involved in their lives." The details and the degree of desperation in many of those letters was truly heartbreaking.

Fortunately other positive, encouraging letters offered hopeful evidence that many guys are getting the message.

For example, in response to a standard follow-up form that asked, "What was your most important action point from this Promise Keepers conference?" one man wrote: "Building a strong family. My family needs me more than ever, and my wife needs my support. My wife needs me to be more involved in disciplining our children and teaching them to respect her as their mother and my wife. I've found that even small changes make huge differences in a marriage."

One wife's response highlighted and celebrated the changes many women say they are seeing in their husbands: "I can't describe the feeling I had when Mike prayed for me the first time! He was thanking God for me and asking for the Lord's blessing and protection over me and our family. It was an extremely meaningful, beautiful, and intimate moment for both of us."

I'm very thankful for such encouraging words of hope, because there remains a great deal of frustration in so many relationships.

I think of a woman I met one time while speaking on the west coast. Let's call her Joan. It didn't take me long to decide this was a wise, sensitive, and insightful woman. Her husband, whom we'll call Frank, has a great heart for serving God. Frank has made ministry the highest, most important mission in his life. In the process, without ever making a conscious choice to do so, he's relegated his family to a lower spot on his totem pole of priorities. They realize it. And all of them are beginning to pay the price.

For years, without complaint, Joan has played the role of a single mom. She's borne the extra load and taken up the slack at home, in order to accommodate Frank's great calling. Over time she's proven so dependable that he's gradually left more and more details of daily life entirely up to her. Dependency became his habit. Weariness and long-suffering became hers. He's now an effective and respected Christian leader with an extensive public ministry, while she's become increasingly frustrated and exhausted playing the dual roles of mother and father at home.

Joan is now a burned-out, middle-aged mother, with three demanding and needy teenaged children. She admits: "I just can't do it anymore. I can't deal with the pressures of life."

But Joan isn't just an example of how frustrated and alone women feel over their lack of parenting support. Her case is representative of a second major frustration women experience: home work.

I'm Not Your Maid

When I say home work I'm not referring to after-class assignments. I'm talking about the constant maintenance, upkeep, and management required by any place of residence. As a serious frustration factor, this closely follows "raising the family" on women's lists of most common complaints.

Why are women angry? For many of us, a primary frustration rests right here. Eighty-five percent of women responding to one recent survey conducted by a leading consumer magazine said they were stuck with the biggest share of household responsibilities. At the same time, most men said they divided up responsibilities 50–50 in their homes. Interestingly enough, this difference in perspectives wasn't only an American phenomenon. Another survey found a similar percentage of Russian women complaining about the same uneven division of household labor.

Women the world over resent the choice we're left with: We have to take care of everything around the house or become the proverbial nag to muster up a fair share of husbandly help. In an attempted alternative to verbal harassment, many of us resort to what is endearingly termed a "honey do" list in hopes that our most pressing household concerns will soon be addressed.

However, most of us are notoriously soft touches. When our loving husband comes home he's emotionally and physically drained from another hard day on the job. Most of us know the feeling. We can't expect him to go till he drops. So we give him a little time and space. Enough hard and demanding days create a serious need for recreation, but then yet another weekend flies by without the necessary chores getting attended to.

Unfortunately, for most families in our culture, there's never enough income to afford the kind of specialized help needed to do either the regular or periodic maintenance projects required to keep a home in tip-top condition. Usually the woman is at home more of the time, facing the many nagging daily reminders of so many needs that it sometimes seems as if her home is slowly, steadily deteriorating before her eyes. The result is often a sense of frustrated powerlessness. And in turn, anger.

That's what happened in the case of Joan and Frank. If she doesn't attend to a household problem, it doesn't get done. Consequently, their longtime home has become in Joan's words, "pretty run-down." For the past two years she admits she's "pretty much given up. I'll take care of my own things and maintain my own personal space and possessions. When I make a mess, I won't leave it; I'll clean up after myself in the kitchen and bathroom. But that's all I can cope with, all I can manage. Frank and the kids are on their own."

Sadly, Joan's teenage children and her husband have never developed the habit of helping because it doesn't seem to matter to them. The kids consider her a nag and an unreasonable heavy when she asks for a little assistance. Frank is seldom there to model a servant attitude or to back up her requests for help with his necessary added authority. So Joan has become a very tired, frustrated, and angry woman.

I know countless women like Joan who are contending with the same basic issues in their families. Why is this so frustrating?

I believe men need to realize that a woman considers her home a direct extension of her identity, a clear and telling reflection of who she is. Whether or not a problem or flaw is any fault of hers, she still feels as if others are going to consider her somehow responsible.

Repeatedly I hear women express through frustrated tears how they are so ashamed of the condition of their homes that they sometimes wish they could just run away from it all. I've had women tell me about being out doing neglected yard work or garage cleanup, and having neighbors call out to them from across the way to ask why their husbands aren't out there helping. Humiliated, they feel compelled to shout back some explanation, any excuse, just to make their husband look better in their neighbors' eyes (if not in their own). All the while they are seething inside and asking themselves: *Why can't I get him out here to help me? Why is his schedule so full that he can't even help me at home? I need rest and recreation too. When is it my turn to sit in front of the TV?*

By this point I suspect some of you guys may be feeling some well-warranted frustration of your own. After all, whoever said only husbands could fulfill the "honey do" list.

And you know what, guys? I realize some of you are not only model parents intimately involved in every area of your childrens' lives, you're accomplished and available jack-of-all-trades who complete household repairs faster than your wives can make out a "to do" list. If your wife indeed has no reason for frustration over your role as "Super-Dad" or "Mr. Fix-It," please don't be too defensive here. Your wife may be feeling frustrated over other issues instead.

The frustration many women experience in the workplace often carries over at home. But there are plenty of other frustrations rooted right at home, in our relationships. Many women, as we'll see in coming chapters, are frustrated about not being listened to or heard, not feeling valued, not being included or even considered. I know women frustrated by the lack of stability and sense of roots in their lives because their husbands are chasing one dream after another. I've watched many a woman grow more and more frustrated as she's waited in vain for her husband to find "meaningful" work and settle on a career path he thinks can lead to fulfillment.

I've seen even more women frustrated when some change she expected to take place in her husband or her relationship never happened.

Even seemingly minor problems and irritating little habits can grow old and frustrating over time. (That goes for men and women.) And any frustration can lead to anger.

FEAR: THE THREAT OF FINANCIAL INSECURITY

Let me share a personal illustration about the way fear nourished my anger.

Randy and I came from such very different backgrounds that, in looking back, I can see that our marriage was an accident waiting to happen. I grew up in an intact family. My dad had a typical military officer's take-charge personality. He always took pride and care in fulfilling his role as family provider. Our family certainly wasn't perfect; indeed, some of my critical emotional needs were never met. But I don't remember ever having a single worry about our family's basic financial affairs because the Army provided a steady monthly income. Though we certainly weren't rich, I grew up with the sense of security that comes from always, and almost automatically, having all my physical needs provided for.

In contrast, Randy's parents split when he was only six. His mother suddenly faced the fearful prospect of raising three children on her own. When Randy's stepfather came into the picture, he gladly married Randy's mom and assumed the responsibility of a ready-made family; but he was only twenty-one and working for minimum wage. So making ends meet was tough for a long time. Home and family may have provided love and a place to belong, but not necessarily a comforting sense of financial security and stability. Growing up, Randy wasn't taught the skills of money management. (For that matter, neither was I.) What he learned instead were survival skills and the fine art of doing what it takes to get by.

I vividly recall an incident that occurred during a visit with Randy's family early in our married life. We were having a family conversation in his folk's living room when we heard a knock at the front door. Immediately everyone grew quiet. Whoever was outside knocked again. I started to ask Randy for an explanation, but he quieted me with a meaningful look. It wasn't until later that Randy helped me understand why no one answered the door.

"When you grow up on a shoestring budget," he explained, "with your folks doing everything they can, well . . . any stranger knocking on the door could be someone trying to collect on past due accounts."

The experience was a real eye-opener for me, particularly Randy's matter-of-fact response. He said nothing more of the incident, but I couldn't get the scene out of my mind.

The difference in our backgrounds didn't create any immediate problems early in our marriage, in part because we were so in love we went through a three-year honeymoon period where we were oblivious to anything and everything but each other. Since Randy was in the service when we met and for some time after we got married, our newlywed, military lifestyle seemed familiar, predictable, and stable.

Our situation changed dramatically, however, once Randy completed his military commitment and decided to enroll in a California Bible college. We signed up for all the usual student loans. I found a job as an assistant manager of an apartment complex, which afforded us a free place to live and some additional income. With a part-time waitressing job, I brought in almost enough income to cover our regular monthly obligations. To make up the difference, Randy agreed to take on a part-time maintenance position at the same complex. It seemed a perfect job for him, with flexible hours he could arrange around his class schedule and study time. But as time went by, schoolwork, campus leadership, and student-community projects took on greater and greater urgency. Randy put in fewer and fewer hours on the job, and I was forced to take on more of the work and financial load.

I saw what was happening and it bothered me, mostly because of the snide comments my manager would make about my "irresponsible husband" when she saw me doing some of Randy's work—jobs such as washing windows and changing lightbulbs around the complex. I'd try to explain that Randy had a test to study for or a big paper to do, and I was glad to help out, but her judgments hurt. It soon became obvious our income wasn't covering our needs, and when I realized I couldn't add any more to my workload, fear began to set in.

Our financial hole grew deeper and deeper until the morning I received a phone call from the utility company telling me they would turn off our electricity the next day if we didn't pay our past due bill. I remember hanging up the phone and walking over to the window, staring helplessly at the ground below, crying because we had no money to pay the bill and feeling absolutely terrified about the future. Anger welled up inside me as I said out loud to an absent husband, "Fine! If you don't take care of me, I'll take care of myself. But you better watch out, and you better stay out of my way!" I'd never had to live that way before. That was the day I kicked into an angry, aggressive survival mode.

If that incident wasn't enough, I can recall an even more disturbing experience during that same time. A single guy, a friend of Randy's, was staying over at our apartment for the night when the doorbell rang at five A.M. Our overnight company got up off the couch to answer it. By the time Randy and I stumbled out of the bedroom, we found our guest in the living room, face-to-face with a repo man who'd come to collect the used VW bug we hadn't made a payment on for a couple months. I don't remember whether Randy gave the guy a check, or if we just happened to have enough cash on hand to satisfy the collector; I do know he left without taking our car.

I was humiliated beyond belief. Randy didn't want me to make an issue of it when we retreated into our bedroom.

But I couldn't believe he'd allowed us to be put in a position like that.

The damage was done by this point. I was clearly getting a very frightening message: Things may have been safe before when I was growing up, but things were definitely not safe now. I couldn't trust Randy to take care of our basic needs. I was embarrassed. I was scared. And I was furious.

A pattern was being established. From that time on, whenever we faced monetary crises in our marriage, whenever we disagreed about financial decisions, whenever Randy brushed off my money concerns with his confident "It'll be okay" attitude, whenever I worried about some unforeseen expense, I fell into the same pattern I established in those starving student days. First I'd worry, *What's going to happen to us?* Then I'd be angry at Randy for letting us fall into a predicament that fostered such fear.

Only in recent years have I been able to forgive Randy and find healing for the fear and anger that crippled our relationship for so long. I now realize Randy neither understood my fear, nor meant to cause it. As he learned to assume more responsibility over the years, as he valued and provided for the security our children and I needed, I've come to realize that he's been learning everything by trial and error. Randy, like his stepfather and like more and more men in modern society who have grown up without a strong father figure in the home, had to operate in the dark, without an instruction manual, until he began to figure it out for himself. This was a long and painful process for us both. In the meantime, I spent many angry, fearful years and learned that our experience wasn't all that uncommon.

Many women are angry because they too are afraid. Of what? Lots of things. Many wrestle as I did with security issues: *What if he doesn't take care of his end of the fiscal responsibilities? What if we end up on the streets?* Health issues: *What if he doesn't start taking better care of himself, drops dead of a heart attack, and leaves the kids and me without his support? What if I get sick, or one of the kids does? Will he be there for me, for us? Will he even know what we need?* Or future uncertainties: *What if something goes wrong and he can't protect us? What if—in this day of easy, no-fault divorce—he simply abandons us?* Women fear a myriad of "what ifs" today. For every woman it's different. Yet for every woman it's the same because that fear easily manifests itself in anger.

PAIN: THE TERRIBLE HURTS OF INFIDELITY AND ABUSE

Even more women may feel angry because they've been hurt—because they have experienced, or are experiencing, great pain. For many women, like me, the pain started early in our lives and came concealed in the emotional baggage we dragged with us into our marriage relationship. Earlier I mentioned the molestation and the date rape I survived as a teen. Those experiences and the subsequent relational garbage I endured affected my marriage. Such a history can and does produce deep and lasting pain. And out of such pain can grow an uncontrollable, irrational, and extremely destructive anger. I know I couldn't begin to manage the anger I was experiencing in my life and in my marriage relationship with Randy until I finally began to face and find healing for those old painful wounds.

Not all the pain angry women feel today is rooted in ancient or childhood history. Much of it has been planted, nurtured, and harvested entirely in the fertile soil of the marriage relationship. Let me share an example I encountered recently.

I was sitting in the backstage tent at a 1996 Promise Keepers conference when I happened to look up and notice a silver-haired, middle-aged man standing thirty feet away at the edge of our roped-off security area. He was watching me. But I was busy, so I lowered my eyes and resumed my careful listening. When the speaker finished and I glanced up, the man was still staring.

A few minutes later one of our volunteers approached me. "Holly," he said. "There's a guy over there who says he'd like to talk to you. He says he knows you." I looked where he indicated. It was the same man. Now it was my turn to stare. *Do I know him?* I certainly couldn't place him.

"Okay," I told the volunteer. "Could you please bring him over?" By this time I was curious.

As the man approached me, he smiled, extended his hand in friendly greeting, and stated his name. I couldn't believe it. I hadn't seen Jeff for years. Randy and I had known Jeff and his wife, Martha, a number of years earlier in another city. Jeff had grayed considerably in the intervening years and was a long way from home at this particular conference—both reasons I hadn't initially recognized him. I invited him to sit down so we could talk.

"What brings you to Los Angeles? What's Martha doing these days? How have you two been?" My sudden salvo of questions conveyed my initial excitement over seeing him again, until Jeff's reaction brought me up short. Tears began to well up in his eyes and spill down his cheeks. This self-made man—a high-level executive in a major corporation, a man who had always been on the emotionally reserved side, someone who was almost macho in his manner toward his wife and her friends—was crying right there in front of me.

Over the next few minutes the story came out. He'd recently gone on an extended overseas assignment for his company. Martha had remained stateside to manage the home front and take care of their three kids. While Jeff was gone he spent an inordinate amount of time working alongside an attractive young female coworker with whom he eventually had an affair. He'd felt so guilty when he returned home that he had confessed his indiscretion to Martha, who was still so upset Jeff said, "I don't know if our marriage will survive!" I listened in a state of shock as this friend poured out his guilt and heartache.

Since I felt he really needed another man to talk to, I asked Coach McCartney if he'd join us. Then I left the two of them alone for a while. When they finished talking and praying a few minutes later, Jeff asked me if I thought Randy and I could meet with him and Martha before we left town. When I explained we were flying out the next day, Jeff proposed we meet in our hotel restaurant for a few minutes before we checked out. "Sure," I told him, looking forward to seeing my old friend, Martha, and at the same time, dreading what I expected would be a very emotional encounter.

I was right. Martha greeted us warmly in our hotel lobby the next day, but above her smile I could read the sadness and pain in her eyes. She'd been badly betrayed and deeply hurt. She was clearly very angry.

Jeff, in contrast, seemed hopeful, as though he were thinking, *Maybe now that Randy and Holly are here, they can get Martha to forgive me, to see the whole picture. And I won't have to go through this torture any longer.*

After the opening pleasantries I figured we might as well jump right in. I informed her that Jeff had told us everything the day before. That from what we could tell, he was genuinely brokenhearted and wanted to see their relationship restored. That's why we were meeting with them, we told her.

By this point, I could practically feel my friend's blood beginning to boil. So we asked her to share their story from her vantage point. She told us pretty much everything he had—with a few "little facts" Jeff had neglected to mention. The woman with whom Jeff had had the affair was calling their house all the time to talk to him; she'd even follow Jeff to his fitness club and talk with him there. When Martha found out this was happening and confronted Jeff, he had promised to break off all contact. Yet it was still going on. Martha told us she'd recently gotten so fed up with the ongoing deception that she'd insisted the "girlfriend" come over so Martha could confront her in Jeff's presence.

Jeff spoke up at this point to tell us that Martha had gotten physical and slugged him while the "girlfriend" was there, and then he added that one reason he'd gotten involved with another woman was because of Martha's volatile emotions—she could explode in anger one minute and become completely distant the next. When he said this I got the distinct impression he was justifying his affair because of Martha's emotional displays. He just couldn't seem to understand why she was so angry.

Jeff did know that Martha had been sexually abused as a teenager by her grandfather. He'd known for years, from talking to Martha and her counselor, that this history caused her to struggle with intimacy and sometimes act distant. Martha told us she'd only recently reached the point in their marriage when she felt she could let down her defenses and be intimate without fear or reservation, and now his infidelity had destroyed the fragile trust she had for Jeff and shattered what self-esteem she'd been able to muster for herself.

Why was she so angry?

Could it have had anything to do with the fact that months had gone by and he still refused to let go of this "friendship" with the other woman. That he'd met this woman on more than one occasion to "break it off once and for all"—but it still hadn't happened.

Randy and I had gone into our meeting expecting to try to help Martha understand her husband's remorse. Instead we spent the entire hour we had together trying to help him recognize Martha's pain—to understand her distrust and anger. To see that he might not ever be able to win back Martha's trust. And that the only hope for their marriage was for him to slam the door tight on his other relationship and never look back. Incredibly, Martha said that was all she wanted or expected.

Jeff couldn't or wouldn't make that promise. It was heartbreaking.

Martha was angry because her trust had been—and was still being—betrayed.

Unfortunately, Jeff and Martha are not alone. In thousands of marriages wives and husbands have felt terribly betrayed. But before you get your defenses up or simply discount the example by declaring, "That's not me! I've never had an affair and would never commit adultery in a million years!" let me respond in two ways.

First, I would caution you not to be so quick to speak. When I read the statistics on how many husbands and wives are unfaithful, when I consider how many times I've been personally shocked and devastated by the infidelity of people I'd least expect to fall into sexual temptation, I realize affair-proof marriages are few and far between.

I'm not being fatalistic. I just urge caution. Peter swore he'd be loyal to Jesus, no matter what. Yet he betrayed Christ. Betrayal certainly isn't inevitable. But our hearts can deceive us. We can be so sure there is no danger that we don't recognize it until we've tripped and fallen.

Second, I would remind you that there are a lot of other ways, other than affairs, in which spouses can feel betrayed. For example, I've known many women who felt betrayed when they discovered the unexpressive, demanding men they ended up married to bore very little resemblance to the attentive, accommodating charmers who courted and wooed them to the altar. *Sometimes* I've had to conclude the deceit was deliberate. More often I think it's simply the combined result of naiveté and a seriously flawed dating game that requires us all to put our best foot forward while downplaying, postponing, or entirely avoiding the need for such crucial relational values as honesty, openness, and vulnerability.

Either way, whether or not the deceit was intentional, it feels like betrayal. That hurts. Dishonesty hurts. Unfulfilled expectations hurt. And anger is often the fruit of such hurt.

Truth be known, there are probably more common causes of pain than of fears. Most of them will seem pretty small compared to the big pain of something like adultery. But the small hurts—the little things done (or not done) that make a woman feel devalued, discounted, or unloved—also add up to anger. And we'll consider some of those specifics, as well as more general patterns of hurtful behavior in upcoming chapters.

LOOK INTO YOUR OWN LIFE

Remember our original question, Why is she so angry? I've tried to answer as honestly as I could—based on my own experience and that of many other women I've encountered. I know we've only scratched the surface of this question. Later chapters will expand on this discussion.

However, I suspect some of you may be feeling a little guilty about what I've said thus far. Others of you may not be sure how much if any of this might apply to your life.

Either way it could be a good time for you to take that hard look at your own relationship, and set aside a block of time in an environment that will allow for a reasonable, two-sided honest attempt to answer the question we've addressed here.

This kind of discussion can be distressing. I know. Randy and I went through an encounter that was initially devastating. We felt so overwhelmed by the depth and complexity of our problems neither of us knew if our marriage would survive. Just reading the following low point in the Phillips' relationship may make you feel overwhelmed and discouraged. But my prayer is that, as you realize how bad things were for Randy and me, you find more encouragement and hope as you learn how different our relationship is today. For this horrible experience became a major turning point in our marriage. Here's our story ...

THE NIGHT OF THE STOPLIGHTS

Soon after that unforgettable lunch when Randy first told me he thought I needed professional help, I sought out a counselor. Not merely because Randy suggested it, but mostly for the sake of my kids. I realized the underlying tone of bitterness and anger I lived with wasn't the example I wanted for them.

It didn't take many sessions to discover the deepest roots of my anger went way back before my relationship with Randy. Much of my pain could be traced back to a pattern of sexual molestation that began when I was young. In finally facing and talking about that horrible period in my life, I began to see that once that happened, I was emotionally vulnerable and primed for the broad pattern of self-destructive behavior I engaged in as an adolescent. Given my circumstances, the worst mistakes of my teenage years were not only understandable, they were predictable and almost inevitable. Still, it took time and emotional energy to understand and work through that part of my personal history.

Eventually I began to identify other issues—difficult relationships, job-related problems—things I considered only indirectly related to Randy and my marriage. Then came the night when I began to complain about a number of things Randy had said or done.

When I finished recounting the first incident, I'll never forget the response of the counselor who was helping me work through these things: "That incident didn't reflect a very loving response on Randy's part."

When I heard those words, a dam suddenly broke somewhere deep in my soul. As much as I wanted to stem the tide, I began to remember and recount one incident after another. Each time the counselor would respond much the same way: "Was that a response of love?" or "That certainly wasn't the response I'd expect from a loving husband." Each time the words hit me like a vicious blow in the pit of my stomach.

To understand the full impact of those comments, you probably need to know a bit of our background. A handful of incidents in the months just prior to Randy's suggestion that I get professional help made me so furious I would actually storm out of the house, jump in the car, peel out of our driveway, and angrily speed away. I never went far—usually only two or three blocks from home, where I'd park at a spot looking out at the foothills. I'd cry out with great hurt and utter frustration to God: "Lord! I don't believe Randy loves me! He's not even a friend to me; if he was my friend he'd have cared enough to want to help me—he wouldn't have said what he just said! He can't possibly like me. What happened, God? Why did he marry me if he doesn't like me?" Those thoughts were so painful, those doubts so terrifying, I could only express them to God at the point of my deepest despair. Then I'd drive back home desperately trying to shut those sentiments completely out of my mind.

And now, here I was laying out the evidence, incident after incident, only to have an objective expert look me in the eye and clearly, deliberately, pronounce a professional judgment echoing my own worst fears: "This doesn't sound like a loving response to me."

The tearful, emotional session finally ended. I walked out of the counselor's office, climbed in my car, and headed home. Instead of turning up the freeway ramp for the usual, easy, thirty-minute drive home, for some reason I opted to take the surface streets from South Denver all the way to our home in a northwest suburb of the city, which on this particular evening meant that I hit a red light every two or three blocks. Every time I braked to a stop, another hurtful memory surfaced—each recollection accompanied by deep wracking sobs and a flood of tears.

The pattern lasted the entire drive. Start, stop, memory, sobs, tears. Start, stop, memory, sobs, tears. By the time I finally pulled into our driveway I was so completely drained—an empty shell—that I barely worked up the energy to stagger inside. Randy was sitting in a living-room easy chair when I opened the front door.

"How'd it go?" he asked.

"It was tough" was all I managed to reply.

"Want to talk about it?" he asked.

"No," I mumbled as I walked on out of the room. He let me go without asking anything else.

A few merciful minutes passed before I heard him call, "Holly, want to come in here for a minute?" I didn't want to, but I did. And I sagged into a seat across the room from my husband.

"What did you two talk about tonight?" he asked. He'd always shown an interest in the progress my counselor and I were making.

I had no tears or rage left. I felt like a total zombie when I told him, without a trace of emotion or expression, in a barely audible monotone: "I don't think you can hear what I have to say, Randy."

Almost as softly he responded, "If I need to hear it, Holly, I need to hear it."

"I feel like I'll be risking everything by talking right now," I told him. "If I do, I'm not sure you and I will ever be the same again."

Randy suddenly got a wide-eyed, almost fearful, look. "Just tell me," he urged. "Tell me."

I sighed in resignation and began. "Do you remember when you ..."

He nodded at the mention of the incident.

I continued matter-of-factly, "I think that may have been the most hurtful thing that ever happened to me in my life."

Randy just listened.

"Do you remember the time ..." He said he did. "Do you know how that made me feel?" I asked. Then I told him.

"Do you remember ... ? Remember the time ... ?" One after another I replayed the incidents I'd remembered at every traffic light on my drive home. Silent tears streamed down my face as I talked. But there wasn't any bite of emotion left in my voice. And Randy just listened as I spilled out—without change of expression, without any of my usual rancor—all the pain I had carried inside me which had fueled those years of anger.

"I thought we were friends, Randy!" I said at one point. He sat stunned into pained silence as I recounted the events of the evening that had brought me face-to-face with the horrible truth that my own husband didn't like me and maybe didn't even love me anymore.

I have no idea how long I went on. But I finally reached the point of telling Randy, "I don't know what else to say. I have no idea where we go from here. All I do know is, this is pretty hard for me to live with right now." Then I stood up and went to bed.

ASKING THE TOUGH QUESTIONS

In upcoming chapters I'll share with you more of the incidents I recalled for Randy on that night of the stop-lights. I will also share Randy's responses and the subsequent chain of events that God has since used to transform both of our lives and our marriage. It was by no means a one-sided story. Stick around.

I know this has been a pretty heavy emotional load to dump on you so far, especially at the beginning of what is meant to be a book resulting in hope and promise. But things get better. Things got better for us! It is not hopeless.

I personally find it very encouraging that so many men have asked me, "Why is she so angry?" in their quest for honest answers. But we all need to be reminded that asking the tough questions is merely step one in the healing process. If we're going to alleviate the obvious anger, if we're going to improve relationships between the genders, we're going to have to listen and thoughtfully respond to each other. And we're going to have to pay attention to the reasons for that anger given in this chapter and throughout the rest of these pages.

SO WHAT DOES SHE WANT FROM YOU, ANYWAY?

She wants you to:

- Understand what frustrates her.
- Help share her load.
- Recognize and ease her fears.
- Respond to her pain.
- Examine your relationship for causes of frustration, fear, and pain.

chapter **2**

How Can She Say I Don't Value Her?

Appreciating the Difference Between What She Does and Who She Is

---

Most of you guys who have been asking me this question are genuinely perplexed. Some of you are feeling defensive.

I hear you saying, "I love her! I value her more than anyone else on earth! She's the most important person in my life! I think she's a wonderful wife and a terrific mother to our kids. How can she think I don't value her?"

To answer that question let me tell you what I've been hearing from other women. Also I'd like to share some personal experiences from the many years in our marriage when it seemed Randy didn't see any value in me.

JUDGED AND FOUND WANTING

I met Sybil and Al Martin on a trip a few years ago. The Martins have been married almost twenty years and worked together every day in Al's family business. The long hours and heavy, unrelenting demands of the company seldom bothered Sybil in the early years of her marriage. It was the price to be paid for success in business, she told herself. It was an investment in the family's future. At least she was working side by side with Al as he taught her everything he knew about this generations-old family venture.

Sybil proved to be such a quick learner and capable businesswoman that Al gradually began relying more and more on his wife to handle the day-to-day details of company administration. He and his three partner-brothers concentrated their efforts on personnel, public relations, and the ongoing development of the business.

Sybil soon became such a crucial part of the operation that when she became pregnant with Al, Jr., the rest of the family convinced her husband that they couldn't afford for her to stay home with the baby. So Sybil found little Al a day-care home and came back to work, against her own wishes, just a few weeks after giving birth.

While the business did continue to grow, so did Sybil's responsibilities and her husband's demands. On those occasions when she broached the subject of easing out of the business in favor of an improved family life, Al was adamant. The best thing they could possibly do for themselves and their family was to make sure the family business flourished. With the struggling economy, they'd have to work more, not less. When Sybil worked up the courage to tell him she didn't think she could do that and suggested they hire a manager to take over her job, Al reluctantly posed the possibility to his partner-brothers. They nixed the idea immediately: "We can't afford to pay anyone to do what Sybil does," they said. "It would take years to teach a new person everything she's learned about this company! We need her!"

So Sybil kept working. Longer and harder. Wishing the whole time she didn't have to.

Sybil's life continued to deteriorate. In recent years, she's developed a rare, potentially life-threatening health condition. Whether or not the physical and emotional stress of the job created the problem, the pressures at work certainly didn't help matters. Sybil's doctors warned that her condition was progressive and that she needed to conserve her strength and energy to fight it. The prognosis so frightened her that she immediately cut way back on her work hours. But within months Al and his family pressured her into reassuming more of her old job. Even her illness didn't end the constant insinuations that she was no longer pulling her weight.

After investing years in the business, Sybil told me, "It suddenly seemed as if I couldn't do anything right. On the one hand, they said they couldn't get along without me. On the other hand, no matter how long or hard I worked, I could never do enough to please my husband or his family."

To make matters worse, the Martins' only son, Al, Jr., now a teenager, became verbally abusive toward Sybil. This has been the most painful indignity she's had to endure. "I can't seem to do enough to please him either," Sybil said.

For years Sybil tried to ignore the problems and her growing sense of inadequacy. "Al's a good Christian man. I still love him," she told me. "But I can't go on like this anymore. I don't think any human being ought to be treated this way. I just don't know what I'm going to have to do to get a little consideration and respect!"

Sybil's circumstances may seem extreme, but her feelings are not. If we're serious in asking, "How can she say I don't value her?" we can gain some important insights from Sybil's story.

KNOW YOUR WORD POWER

I talk to women on a regular basis who, like Sybil, feel they are constantly being scrutinized and found wanting by the most important people in their lives—their husbands or their bosses. In some cases, the criticism could qualify as verbal abuse, but usually it's more subtle than that.

Sometimes it's offered in the form of *constructive criticism*: "Next time why don't you ..." or "If I could make one small suggestion ..." or "You know it would really have been better if ..." Second-guessing may be the most subtle judgment of all: "Why did you ... ?" or "Did you ever think about ... ?"

If these questions were asked infrequently, it would be no big deal. They would probably warrant attention and serious consideration. But when they are asked on a frequent, regular basis, over time, any person subjected to such patterns of judgment (severe or mild) will feel devalued.

If too much negative feedback results in many women feeling devalued, too little positive feedback can produce much the same problem. You don't have to read too far between the lines of Sybil's story to see how desperate she was for affirmation from her husband. And you don't have to talk to very many women to discover numbers of them who feel the same way—not so much out in the workplace (only a few women work with their husbands professionally), but certainly at home.

One of the most common stresses for women is that we aren't given any formal written job description for our roles as wives and mothers. We do receive a world of advice—much of that contradictory. Every husband, mother-in-law, friend, and stranger in the grocery store has his or her own ideas on what we should be doing differently. But unlike a workforce job, mothers and homemakers receive no regular structured evaluations or annual job reviews, and therefore little, if any, planned opportunity for encouragement and positive feedback. In addition, the job of homemaking comes without opportunity for promotion, with no annual raises, and without even a salary—which we know is how the rest of the world usually measures value.

Finally, mothering entails a sometimes overwhelming sense of responsibility that can be difficult to handle.

Is it any surprise then that so many women, including many who find a great sense of accomplishment, success, and fulfillment in their outside careers, feel unaffirmed and taken for granted at home?

WHO SHE IS, NOT WHAT SHE DOES

At this point in our conversation I can imagine many of you are saying what I hear from guys all the time: "Wait a minute! I'm not one to be critical. I try never to take my wife for granted. In fact, I recognize and appreciate everything she does for me. And I make a point of telling her, on a regular basis!"

I'm always glad to hear that. And yet, even in those cases, some women still feel devalued.

Why?

A key may lie in what one man admitted to me: "I guess the truth is, I appreciate her because she does so much stuff that benefits me. I do value her. But I value her for what she *does*, more than for who she *is*."

This is sad. Until more of us understand the difference between valuing a woman for what she *does* versus who she *is*, we'll never be able to adequately answer the question we're addressing here: "How can she say I don't value her?"

Here's an illustration.

LOVE ME, LOVE MY MUSIC

In those early honeymoon years of our marriage, I never doubted Randy's love for me. I felt he appreciated my talents. We'd actually met at a Waikiki coffeehouse where he came and heard me sing. And after we were married, when we'd have company in our home, Randy would often encourage me to pull out my guitar and then sit there proudly watching and listening to me sing for our guests. His evident pride and enjoyment of my voice and guitar always made me feel respected and valued.

That began to change however after Randy became a pastor. Then he needed me to play the role of a pastor's wife. I didn't fit that mold very well. Since I hadn't really grown up in the church, I wasn't even sure what that mold was, which meant that Randy, who hadn't grown up in a church either, developed his own ideal image of a pastor's wife. And it wasn't me!

The ideal was somebody much quieter and more soft-spoken. Much less opinionated and more tactful. Much less visible and more reserved. Much less aggressive and more genteel. Much less demonstrative and more ... well, you get the idea. Like a movie director instructing a cast member, over the years, Randy very clearly let me know that he wanted me to tone down my personality—to alter or repress the person I really was—in order to better play my new role of pastor's wife. He never said as much in words. But the clear and silent assumption was that I needed to give up my true self, or at least disguise myself behind the image of the ideal pastor's wife, which he, or in some cases his colleagues, expected me to portray.

I can't count the number of times we'd be eating with associates or parishioners when I'd start to tell a story, express an opinion, or share an idea I had—only to feel Randy touch my leg or nudge me under the table in a silent warning that he suspected what I was about to say would be inappropriate or unappreciated. He got where he could even silence me from across a crowded room with an almost imperceptible shake of the head or a split second of eye contact accompanied by a slightly raised eyebrow.

Randy was careful not to embarrass me publicly. And I never wanted to make a scene, though sometimes I came dangerously close. I was definitely walking a tightrope! I'd shut my mouth, retreat into silence, and seethe inside.

Such incidents devalued me as a person and led to serious problems in our marriage. They also inflicted new and serious wounds. After all, if Randy didn't value my input, that clearly meant he didn't value me. If Randy didn't value or trust my judgment, why should I?

NO FEAR?

Another reason I didn't feel Randy valued me was because it seemed he didn't always value the things that concerned me. In fact, he routinely minimized, downplayed, or even ignored my worries and fears.

I now understand why he reacted this way. He didn't know what to do. He felt completely powerless to help me solve my problems or relieve my fears. But Randy's lack of response to my very real concerns not only served to belittle them, it also belittled *me*.

One of the most memorable examples had to do with the fear of flying I developed during the early years of our marriage. I never understood what started it; I'd experienced no such trauma over flying when I was growing up. But the problem eventually mushroomed into a real phobia.

The moment I walked into the cabin of a plane the claustrophobia would begin to close in on me. I'd become so panicky I'd have to raise my feet off the floor to keep from feeling the vibration of the engines. Every time I detected a change in the rpms, a shift in power, or an alteration of thrust I'd be convinced we were going down.

Randy lived with these panic attacks for years; I was such a trial for him. Every time we got on a plane I'd say, "Randy, please hold my hand!" Then I'd grab onto him so tightly my knuckles would turn white. I'd plead, "Pray for me." And he would.

Then he'd have to lean over and get right in my face, like a Lamaze coach attempting to establish a focal point, to get my mind off the fear and onto him as he tried futilely to reassure me, "It's gonna be okay. You can do this. We'll make it."

"I know that," I'd tell him. "But can you just keep holding my hand and praying?"

I would wear the poor guy out. (I was not easy to live with.)

I'll always remember the trip Randy and I took to England a few years back. I wanted to go. I even felt we should go. Yet for weeks ahead of time I dreaded the very thought of a ten-hour transcontinental flight.

As usual, when we got on the plane I asked Randy if he'd please pray for me. "Okay!" he agreed in a tone that seemed to me more resigned than compassionate or even interested. He then offered what I can only describe as a "cursory" prayer, told me "It's going to be okay," then shifted in his seat in such a way that he effectively turned his back toward me, and promptly fell soundly asleep.

I couldn't believe it. How could he do that when his wife was so tormented? I spent the entire flight reading my Bible and praying that God would take away my terror— sitting turned toward the window in hopes no one else would notice my tears or panic.

I felt scared and angry. I remember telling God, *I wish you were here in the flesh. I could sit in your lap and let you comfort me. I need someone to hold me right now.* I was so disappointed that my husband didn't take my fears seriously enough to even stay awake with me. By downplaying my fears, he also devalued me.

STOP THE MUSIC

Eventually I recognized what I took as yet another clear indication that Randy no longer respected me for who

I was. And this may have been worse than concluding that my husband didn't value my opinions and input and didn't care about my greatest fears. I came to the disturbing conclusion that Randy didn't even value my talents anymore. This is one of the hurtful memories I recalled on that "night of the stoplights."

Randy was proud of my musical ability in our early years together. He'd always appeared eager and pleased to have me sing or help with the music ministry in the church. And I know he was excited and happy for me in 1981 when I recorded an album with a contemporary Christian music label. When the album was released Randy even took a four-week sabbatical so he could go on tour with me and help take care of our first son, Timothy, who was a toddler at the time. But all that history was called into question after one telling incident that convinced me Randy's supportive attitude toward my music had changed somehow over the years.

I was performing an evening concert for a church audience of mostly senior citizens. From the platform I could see the faces and read the response of my listeners. Everything told me that the crowd was enjoying the music and the concert was going well. Everything, that is, except Randy.

My husband had stationed himself in the very back of the church. He stood where he could watch me and where I could clearly see him. I noticed fairly early in the concert that he seemed restless. And I knew him well enough to suspect why. He was concerned about the age of the audience and worried that maybe my contemporary style of music might not be that well received. But while I'd been concerned about that at the start and had consciously toned down my approach, the positive response I received from the crowd soon freed me up to perform my usual program.

As the evening progressed, Randy evidently failed to pick up the same sense I did. He became even more restless. Then he began motioning at me from the back of the church—by drawing his hand across his throat in a very obvious "cut" sign.

I found it so disconcerting to have my husband calling for a sudden end to my concert that I tried not to look at him during my last two or three songs. While I did manage to keep singing, I began to wonder if maybe something else was going on or if I was completely misreading the situation.

"What was bothering you so much?" I asked when Randy joined me at the door after the concert.

Before he had time to answer, the people from the audience were there, filing past us. But I could see the answer in the surprised look on Randy's face as one person after another stopped to say how much they had enjoyed the concert. As one elderly woman went on and on saying how much my music had moved her, I made eye contact with Randy and smiled. While I was feeling validated by this woman's words, I was also saddened to wonder: *Why am I hearing this from a woman I don't even know? Why doesn't my husband see me this way?*

I could only conclude that Randy didn't truly value my ability to read an audience. Translated, that meant he didn't value *me*.

WHAT'S IN A NAME?

How can she say I don't value her?

If she's like me, she says this after she's carefully weighed some very telling evidence that says her husband doesn't regard her ideas, her concerns, or her abilities.

What made this conclusion so hurtful in my case was that the feedback I was receiving loud and clear from my husband merely reinforced a message I'd been getting all my life. It may have started with the mistreatment I suffered as a girl. The dating scene where women are often treated like sex objects conveyed the same judgment. Then I felt much the same way when I became a pastor's wife—a mere accessory to my husband's career.

Whenever I rewound the memory tapes to replay any of those life experiences, I kept picking up the same old underlying theme, like some back-masked message planted in the background music of my life. *Holly is worthless. Holly doesn't measure up. Holly is bad.*

I'd been invalidated for so long that I'd come to believe my name was very fitting. Like the holly bush, I was so personally prickly—loud, obnoxious, and pushy—that I put people off.

Fourteen years into our marriage I finally began to see myself, and even my name, in a different light. During a Christian women's retreat we were attending, a friend of mine was awakened in the middle of the night with the distinct impression (which she felt was from God) that she needed to study my name and tell me what it really meant.

When we got back home, she went straight to the library, and for the next week, she spent every moment she could spare researching my name. Some weeks later, she came to tell me what she'd done and why. She'd managed to collect more than twenty pages of notes she wanted to share.

The highlights that stuck in my mind are these: The root of the word *holly* can be traced back to ancient Sanskrit, which is considered a very poetic language. The holly bush is considered a beautiful and decorative plant—a hardy evergreen that can bloom all year round. Wood from the holly bush is extremely hard—used only by the best woodworking craftsmen in the very finest and most expensive German inlay work. It is also used to create fine musical instruments. While the hardness of its wood makes the trunk and branches seem strong and tough, a very sweet honey runs through its heart. The holly honey was used as a ceremonial hot drink or as a medicine to rid the body of impurities.

My friend continued, gently sharing what she'd researched about my name and what she felt her findings confirmed about me. As I accepted her warm, kind words as her affirmation (and God's) of me, I felt my spirit being slowly inflated like an inner tube that's been flat and forgotten over a very long, cold winter. I began to cry out of joy and gratitude for this rich verbal blessing, but also out of frustration and sorrow that my husband didn't yet see me this way.

VALUE LOST

For so much of our marriage I never even thought of myself in the context of value. My focus was not turned on me, but rather on Randy—his needs, his job, his value, his present and future calling, and what I needed to do to help him get his work done. It took years for me to become painfully aware that my own feelings, my own opinions, my own fears and insecurities, my own personal desires and dreams, my intrinsic worth as a woman with a good mind, good ideas, good intuition, and valuable skills had been lost and were not even part of the value equation.

I now understand that Randy didn't set out to disregard me or discount my worth. He was oblivious to the fact that value was an issue. In his early childhood family, he hadn't seen a strong marriage model that displayed a measurable respect for the woman.

My own poor communication and problem-solving skills exacerbated the problem in our marriage. I was so out of touch with my own sense of self-worth I never articulated my sense of feeling devalued.

Somewhere inside I was always angry because I was so hurt and frustrated about feeling unimportant and invisible. But instead of addressing the issue directly, I'd simply allow the irritating disregard to continue until I got angry enough to blow a gasket, lash out, and achieve no positive results. I'd manage only to prompt my husband to turn a deaf ear and make my children tremble with fear.

Only by the grace of God did our marriage survive.

Many couples whose marriages don't survive find this value issue at the heart of the problem. In fact, as I conclude this chapter, I have in front of me a very sad letter from a man who admits he didn't consider these questions until it seemed too late. Only after his wife left him did he begin to understand her true value. He summed up his sense of loss in the following words that are part prayer-poem, part heart-cry:

O God, where is my right side?
The one that I fell in love with when I was young.

O God, where is my right side?
The one I married, the one you said was bone
*   of my bone, flesh of my flesh.*
(And I took for granted.)

O God, where is my right side?
The one who has the beautiful smile and laugh.
(I never told her every day.)

O God, where is my right side?
The one who wished to talk and wanted me to listen.
(But football games, friends, and family were too
*   important.)*

O God, where is my right side?
The one who wanted me to hold her hand and put my
*   arm around her.*
(Not just as a prelude to sex.)

O God, where is my right side?
The one who loved you and prayed over our family.

*(I didn't lift her up in prayer or jump for joy when she
    felt your loving touch.)*

O God, where is my right side?
The one who wanted to be a wife and mother.
*(Not the breadwinner and part-time father who
    handled the bills alone.)*

O God, where is my right side?
The one who finally got tired and left.
*(Because I couldn't or wouldn't be the man she
    wanted me to be.)*

O God, where is my right side?
I look for her in the now-empty recesses of my life.
*(Not wanting to admit that I just didn't value her
    the way you wanted me to.)*

Oh God, where is my right side?
*I know in my heart I found her once, in the wife
    of my youth.*
And I know I can't win her back without you.
So I pray for a second chance.
*I hope that a spark of the love she once had
    for me still burns*
*And I pray that the fire of our love might blaze
    once more*
*Ten times greater than before
    so that our lives together will be*
A powerful witness for you. Amen.

HOW CAN SHE SAY I DON'T VALUE HER?

If you've ever asked that question, let me summarize
and bring the heart of this discussion into focus by asking
you a few very pertinent questions. Do you value her as a
person or do you merely value her for what she does for

you? Do you value her only because she is a good wife to you, a good mother to your children, a good homemaker? Have you given any thought to her value *apart* from what she does for you?

How much do you love your wife as a person? Enough? A lot? Immeasurably?

Have you ever even thought about it?

SO WHAT DOES SHE WANT FROM YOU, ANYWAY?

She wants you to:

- Affirm what she does, but more importantly,
- Affirm who she is.
- Receive and validate her emotions.

chapter 3

What Does She Mean When She Says, "It's Always Been About You"?

Recognizing and Rethinking Your Priorities

The outset of Randy's professional ministerial career brought a sudden and definite end to our honeymoon years. And a big part of the growing tension in our relationship centered on the very issue we're addressing here. Let me tell you about those days.

When some old friends from Hawaii came to California to invite us to help them start a new church in the islands, we didn't take the request lightly. After much serious thought, discussion, and prayer, Randy left the Bible college where he was studying, and we moved back to Honolulu. For a young married couple still relatively new to each other and to our faith, this opportunity to do Christian work in a tropical paradise was exciting. We were also going home to where we'd met. But neither Randy nor I had a clue about what our new life in a church-planting ministry would require of us.

The new church had no budget for salaries. So Randy and the other two pastors all had outside jobs. Randy worked during the week as a waiter in a Waikiki restaurant. I landed a job selling puka shells (remember them?) and gold (go figure that combination!) with a local jewelry company. But even with both of us working, we struggled to make ends meet in Hawaii's tourist-price economy.

Only looking back can we see that the financial hardships were minor stresses compared to the heavy work and time demands of our jobs with the church. As one of our congregation's worship leaders, I spent countless hours each week helping plan services and practicing music. In addition to his waiting tables, Randy spent much more time on church work than I did—in meetings with the other pastors, counseling, crisis management, studying, and preparing for his responsibilities as one of the church's teaching pastors. On top of his two jobs, Randy soon decided to continue his formal education by enrolling as a part-time student at a local seminary.

As a result, we had even less time than we had money. But I believed both sacrifices were simply part of the price required by Randy's call into the ministry. So I gladly endured them—for a time.

I remember, however, the growing sense of irritation I'd feel every week after our services when someone needing help would pull Randy aside to discuss a personal or spiritual problem. While they talked, I'd be sitting off to the side or out in the car waiting—a half hour, an hour, sometimes longer. And I'd be thinking, *My husband is spending more time talking with this person than he and I have had alone for the past week.* By the time Randy would be ready to go, I'd be so angry that I couldn't enjoy the time we did have. Then I'd feel really guilty about resenting the demands of a ministry I truly believed God had called Randy to do.

Another major tension point in our marriage began a year or so into our time back in Hawaii. We'd been married for three years, and I really wanted to begin a family. Randy didn't believe we had the resources—either time or money—to think about having a baby. To cap off his argument, he told me he didn't think it was God's plan that we start a family yet. If this were true, I couldn't understand why God had instilled in me such an intense desire for children.

We argued this issue off and on for months and eventually years without making any significant headway. I became discouraged and resentful, thinking, *With both Randy and God teaming up against me, what chance do I have?* Then I'd feel guilty again for feeling that way when God was definitely blessing our ministry efforts with an exciting, growing young church. My feelings of resentment didn't disappear (they just went into hiding) after Randy and I finally had our first child, Timothy, five years into our marriage.

Things were going so well with the Honolulu church by the time Tim was born that the pastors and other leaders decided it was time to try to plant a new sister church in another town on the island of Oahu called Aiea. While I loved that area and looked forward to moving there, and while I was proud and pleased that Randy was to be senior pastor of the new congregation, I also dreaded the time and energy demands I now knew would be required to establish yet another church. And my concerns soon proved to be justified.

Randy so totally committed himself to the launching of this new work that it seemed we had no life of our own. I didn't even feel we had a home of our own. Since the church in Aiea owned no property and used an elementary school for Sunday worship, most of the church's remaining activities took place in our home (which we were already sharing with two single men who helped us with the rent). Bible studies, prayer meetings, and planning sessions became a regular part of our home life. This meant I had visitors, some of whom I barely knew, in my home many nights of those weeks.

The endless stream of company would have been stressful enough. But what really began to grate on me was that as our church members felt more and more at home *in* our home, it was common to find people helping themselves from our kitchen cabinets and refrigerator.

Neither did it seem to matter that I had a baby who needed his rest. Many times people would stand in the hall right outside his bedroom door carrying on conversations until eleven or twelve o'clock at night with no consideration at all of our infant son. We had no privacy and precious little time for family life.

But I still loved Randy very much. And I was very willing to put up with all this and do whatever else I could to be supportive of him and his work. But frequently I felt Randy was married more to his work than he was to me. And that made me jealous, frustrated, and angry.

TROUBLE IN PARADISE

At the release of my album in the spring of 1981, Randy pleasantly surprised me by deciding to take time off to accompany me on tour. We both desperately needed a break from the unrelenting pressures of ministry. Although touring the country with a toddler in tow (and discovering I was pregnant with our second) while performing almost every day wasn't exactly a relaxing vacation, it was a refreshing change of pace. At least Randy and I were together most of each day devoting significant attention to each other and to Timothy's needs.

By the end of the tour, the positive response to the album and our weeks of quality family time had rejuvenated me. Even though my pregnancy was taking its toll, I was feeling encouraged and once again ready to return to the islands and resume my support of Randy in ministry. But life as we knew it was going to take a radical turn. While in Colorado, on the first leg of our tour, Randy came to an unshakable conviction that he was to resign as senior pastor and look for a position where we could be mentored and receive more significant training. He wanted to make the transition a gradual one, but no sooner had we arrived back in Hawaii than we were emotionally ambushed by a double-barreled blast.

Barrel one hit us the first day back home when I got word that my father had died of lung cancer, which had only been diagnosed a few months before. I was unable to return to Virginia for his funeral due to our lack of funds and what had become a precarious pregnancy strained further now by this horrible news of my dad's death.

Barrel two: Only a week after Randy announced to his staff his intent to resign within six months, he received a phone call from the elders of the church inviting him to a special meeting.

Randy looked shell-shocked when he walked back into our apartment after the meeting. "What's wrong?" I wanted to know.

"The elders just asked me to resign."

"They what?" I couldn't believe I'd heard him correctly.

"The elders of the church asked me to resign," he replied. "They take issue with the state of our marriage and feel I'm no longer fit to be a pastor."

While we'd been on the mainland touring for the album, Randy's assistant had evidently concluded that we had a lousy marriage and were poor examples to the people we were supposed to be leading, which in turn meant Randy wasn't fit to be senior pastor of the church. Evidently the elders concurred, because at the meeting they asked for Randy's resignation immediately, citing our marriage, and saying my lack of sensitivity and lack of support for my husband disqualified us from church leadership. It was a cold, impersonal meeting that left Randy feeling numb.

I hadn't even been invited to attend the meeting with my husband—so I was denied the chance to face our accusers. I had no opportunity even to hear, confirm, or deny the accuracy of the private comments now publicly attributed to me.

I was sick. "What are we going to do? What did you tell them?"

For a moment I wasn't sure Randy had even heard me. I guess he was just having trouble getting the words out. "I don't know what we'll do," he finally managed to say. "I asked them for a little time so we could talk and think and pray."

We called a friend to watch Timothy, and the two of us drove across the island in our VW bug and checked into a hotel where we could be alone. We were both too sick in spirit to think about eating. So we spent the next day and a half fasting, talking, praying, and weeping. After investing so much of ourselves in founding the new church, we both felt so deeply hurt by what felt like the betrayal of friends that we just couldn't imagine any course of action that seemed right to us. From our hotel we called an older pastor friend in Colorado who listened to our story and advised, "Get out as soon as you can."

On the one hand, I couldn't help blaming myself for this whole unpleasant mess. If I hadn't complained about the demands of Randy's ministry, no one could have accused me of being an unsupportive wife, and Randy wouldn't have been asked to step down.

On the other hand, I felt my frustrations were legitimate. While I loved Randy very much, I still secretly resented him for having had so little regard for my needs as a wife and mother when he had ample time for all the people in the church who needed him. Because I saw little prospect of my husband or the demands of his career ever changing, I had little hope for our future. I had failed my husband (and God) so miserably, and had been so deeply hurt in the process, that what I thought about doing, what I really wanted desperately to do, was to take our son, leave Randy, and go home to live with my mother.

The only thing keeping me from doing just that was the sobering conviction in my heart that it would be wrong. I believed in the vows we had taken. I loved Jesus and didn't want to do anything that would besmudge his reputation. To leave Randy would mean turning my back on my faith and everything I believed in. And I could never do that.

So I stayed.

COLORADO LOW

We sold virtually everything we had and left Hawaii less than two months later. We bought plane tickets to Colorado where we had no prospects for a job and knew no one other than the pastor friend who'd advised us to leave Hawaii. His church put us up in a hotel for a week, and then one of his church members offered to let us stay at his house until we found something more permanent. Within two weeks we'd rented a cheap apartment, and Randy landed a job loading cans of paint onto pallets on the dock of a Benjamin Moore warehouse.

I'd never seen Randy so discouraged. His dreams had been shattered. Months before he had had the responsibility of a fulfilling new ministry that challenged his faith and demanded every ounce of his emotional, intellectual, and spiritual resources; now he was stuck doing backbreaking menial labor without any prospect of a ministry position in sight. And while he never openly blamed me, I couldn't help feeling very responsible for the deep valley of discouragement in which we found ourselves.

The unquestionable highlight of those following months was the birth of a second son we named Christian. But the indescribable joy we experienced at his arrival so contrasted with our overall state of being that we quickly plummeted back into the emotional sinkhole of our everyday existence.

For over a year we scraped by on the sweat of my husband's brow and the generosity of Christian friends—until Randy was offered a staff position at the church we were attending. Things slowly began to look up again. At least for Randy. I wasn't so sure about me.

The ministry challenges posed by an associate pastor position in an established church proved different from what Randy had experienced as senior pastor of a brand-new congregation in Hawaii. But the demands of the job—in terms of time, energy, and commitment—seemed all-too-familiar to me. We had walked away from our dreams in the paradise of Hawaii, had been exiled for more than a year in professional purgatory, and survived hellish emotional and financial hardship.

For what? Yet another situation where I would be expected to silently endure anything and everything for the sake of Randy's job?

The answers to these questions were made disturbingly clear by an episode that occurred only a year or so into Randy's new ministry position. Once again it was my mouth that provoked the incident. I had said something to a staff member's wife that I see now (from a more seasoned and, I hope, more mature perspective) came across as critical and judgmental. When she took offense and went to her husband with it, he called our home.

Randy and I were about to retire for the night when the phone rang. Randy picked up the extension on our nightstand. When the caller, whose voice he instantly recognized, asked, "May I speak with Holly, please?" Randy handed the receiver across the bed to me.

For the next five minutes Randy sat silently on the edge of our bed listening curiously to my end of what turned out to be a very one-sided tirade. In no uncertain terms, the caller told me I had no right to say what I'd said to his wife. I tried in vain to slip an apology past his angry barrage of words. But each time I started to respond to something he said, he practically shouted me down. He told me I should be glad my husband even had a job, and I should be careful not to jeopardize it. He called me immature and insensitive, and I don't remember what else. All I recall was that long before my husband's colleague finished berating me, I felt he had questioned everything from my basic intelligence, to my character, to my integrity, to the validity of my own personal Christian experience. Stunned by this unexpected verbal assault and battery, finally unable to absorb any more, I silently handed the receiver back to my puzzled husband and collapsed onto the bed in tears. Without a question or word in my defense, Randy bid the man a hasty good-bye and hung up.

"What was that all about?" he asked me.

So I told him. But even there in the privacy of our bedroom, my husband didn't rise to my defense. He tried to comfort me, but I couldn't help sensing he was concerned about the potential implications for his job, and those concerns tempered his response to the way I had been treated. As far as I knew, Randy never discussed the incident or ever even mentioned it to the man who called me.

It took a long time to forgive him for what appeared to be such a complete lack of support. In fact, this was another of those incidents I brought up on the night of the stoplights.

For the sake of my husband and his ministry at that church, I swallowed my pride and later apologized for the comments that had prompted the whole affair. But it seemed the damage was already done.

I eventually took an active role in the women's programs of the church and also offered my musical talents and input in worship. However, after that incident, I never again felt as if my contribution or my viewpoints carried much weight in the ministry of our church. On several occasions I wanted to meet with everyone involved to express my feelings and get the issue out in the open, but Randy always discouraged that idea. He never wanted to run the risk of confrontation. Nor did he want me to say anything for fear it might affect his job.

The rules were well established. If I didn't meet up to the expectations of others, or if I made a mistake because of immaturity, I received anger or rejection in return. Never had there been a time where I felt the security of knowing I could make mistakes and have someone lovingly correct me or show me how old patterns could be broken with the kind of wisdom that comes from caring.

As a result, over the course of time Randy ministered in that church, I felt so increasingly stifled, so insignificant, so abandoned and disregarded (even by my husband) that I occasionally look back on those discouraging days as my ten-year personal dungeon experience. In sacrificing my dreams, my personality, and my very identity on the altar of Randy's career, I came to feel invisible.

And while Randy could honestly say he never asked me to do that, it seemed to be expected. More by the people around my husband than by Randy himself.

HIS AND HER DREAMS

At a business meeting in a restaurant not long ago I told some folks about these struggles I've just recounted. When I described the long discouraging years when I'd lived without any goals of my own, without any real vision or personal dreams for the future, I noticed one of the men at the table had grown particularly quiet. I thought I saw tears welling up in his eyes.

Our discussion soon moved on to other topics, but the next time I saw him, this hard-driving, middle-aged, professional man explained why he'd been so moved by my story. "I saw and heard my wife's pain in your words, Holly," he confessed. "I'd never stopped to think about how much I had expected her to sacrifice on my behalf. I wasn't aware of it before, but our marriage was a classic example of 'it's always been about me.'"

He said God had used my story to convict him—to show him their marriage, their family, their entire lives had been built around his practice, his career, his desires, his dreams. He realized he hadn't ever considered what personal aspirations his wife had set aside to accommodate his drive to "conquer the world."

Listening to me talk, he had come to the sudden, startling realization that his wife had her own feelings, her own needs, her own desires and dreams. He didn't even know what they were. But he'd decided during our dinner conversation, that in appreciation of the many sacrifices she'd made for him through the years, he was going to go home and discover what hopes and feelings his wife had bottled up inside for so long. Then he intended to help her pursue her greatest dreams.

The trouble was, the old pattern had gone on for so long that when he'd determined to change it, his wife didn't know how to respond. "I don't think she completely trusts my motives," he reported sadly. "She can't believe I've really changed. Instead of feeling a new sense of freedom I want her to have, she seems to be looking over her shoulder, just waiting and watching for the other shoe to drop."

ONE-MAN SHOW

How about this story of another middle-aged couple.

The wife is a quiet and introverted woman who for years abandoned herself, her needs, and her identity to a man who demanded (by sheer force of his personality) all the limelight. Only recently has she blossomed and matured into a person courageous enough to venture out of her shell. At first the change threatened and unnerved her husband. But because he is a man with integrity and has a heart that truly wants to do right, he slowly forced himself to break free of old habits and learn to accept and value his wife—openly, through actions as well as words. He prefers her, gives her the floor, and encourages her to express herself, even when it could put him in a less-than-perfect light.

He's still learning, because those old habits die hard. When he's recounting a story or telling about a business trip they have taken to another country he still thinks in the "I" mode—"I went ... I saw ... I did" when, in fact, it was the two of them, he *and* his wife, doing all these things. But she is beginning to bring this old routine to his attention: "You didn't do that alone, honey. You did it with me"; "You didn't take that trip by yourself, we both went." Refusing to disappear into the woodwork any longer, this woman is tenaciously determined to help her husband quit thinking in terms of "I" and begin acknowledging the "we." He's slowly learning that life isn't only about him. He's growing. She's growing. They and their story are heading for a happy ending.

THE COACH'S CASE

Let's consider one last story of a couple who have become very close to Randy and me over the past six years. Coach Bill McCartney, the founder of Promise Keepers, told the story in his own words at the beginning of this book. But it's an example worth reexamining here because the

McCartneys' experience is every bit as pertinent to our discussion as the others I've told.

Remember Bill telling how a guest speaker at their church challenged the men to judge their effectiveness and success by looking into the faces of their wives? When Bill did that, what he saw in his wife Lyndi's eyes was incredible sadness. Within days Coach Mac resigned from his job as head football coach of the University of Colorado.

He suddenly realized that for the entire thirty-two years he'd been coaching football, his wife had structured her life and their family life around him and his job. For years Lyndi McCartney used to carry blankets, pack lunches, and bring her children to sit on the sidelines during football practice—so the kids could at least see their daddy a few minutes each day. "Our entire family life was like that," she told me. "On Sundays we even decided what church services to attend based on when Bill needed to have a coaches' meeting."

But after Bill noted the sadness in Lyndi's eyes, when he realized the damage done by living life to accommodate his own ambition and agenda, he not only decided to resign, he made other drastic changes as well. For the remainder of his final season, he drew a line and told his assistant coaches there would be no meetings after six P.M. He made them go home to their wives and families instead. It was such a foreign concept, that according to Bill, "Some of the guys didn't seem to know what to do!"

When Bill tried to explain his prime motivation for resigning at the peak of his career from one of the premier coaching positions in all of college football, the press simply didn't believe him. Surely, they thought, he was expecting an even better coaching offer in the near future. Or maybe his wife was suffering a serious illness. Or maybe he was just emotionally burned-out and wouldn't admit it. Whatever. The idea that he was giving up his career to strengthen his marriage, that his decision was made in response to the needs of a wife who had sacrificed so much for him over the years, seemed entirely too preposterous for most sports reporters to believe. So off they went speculating—some still do to this day.

ME OR WE?

I don't intend what I'm about to say to be taken as angry or critical judgment. I offer it as a simple observation—something a lot of the men I've talked to admit is true. *When most men consider or pursue goals, desires, or success, they don't usually think in terms of "us." The typical man thinks in terms of "me." And in his mind, if only in his subconscious, the woman in his life is there to help him reach his goals.*

Speaking for women, I would like men to understand that living as if life revolves around you is counterproductive, because it puts men and women at odds with each other. It can prevent husbands and wives from enjoying emotional intimacy. For men who aren't married, it may prevent them from enjoying a positive, *respectful* coexistence with female associates on the job, *and* with other women in their lives. The women at the office aren't there just for the men; they have needs—they have families, weekends, hopes, dreams, goals, plans, and so on.

If men see women as equally entitled to all that life has to offer, it may just be possible for both genders to enjoy an incredible life of powerful harmony.

Why don't more guys understand these truths? Could part of the explanation be that men and women are simply wired differently? Do more males of our species come preprogrammed with a propensity for rugged individualism and a consuming drive for achievement while most women just naturally place a higher priority on relationships? How much of this attitude is learned? If all a guy sees modeled for him as he grows up is the-world-revolves-around-men assumption, it might not even cross his mind that he should give this issue a second thought. Would he even know it *was* an issue? If he doesn't, he may see problems in his relationships with women, but without recognizing the root of the problem, never be able to find any effective solutions.

Whatever the cause, I've become convinced that most men aren't truly aware they have these attitudes. Because it's more subconscious, it should be a little easier for us women to forgive. And it makes me a little more hopeful that men will be eager to help correct the problem once they do recognize it. That's what I've seen happen over and over again in the lives of men with whom I've talked (and cried).

I'm encouraged by the men who are honestly seeking to understand the issues we're discussing here. I'm even more encouraged by those men (like my husband, Bill McCartney, and the other two men whose stories I've just told) who have been taking a long hard look at their own attitudes and have determined to make serious changes where they feel they've been wrong.

At the same time, I'm discouraged that so many wives (including all those in the stories I've recounted) have had to wait until their middle age to benefit from their husbands' changing attitudes. While I can say from personal experience, "Better late than never," one of the motivations for writing this book is to help keep other women from having to endure the years of discouragement and heartache women like my dear friend Lyndi and I have known—when our entire lives seemed to revolve around our husbands' careers.

LEADING BY SERVING

Many Christian men have misused the apostle Paul's instruction to husbands and wives. They wield Ephesians

5:22–24 like a club to demand respect and authority as they quote it: "Wives, submit to your husbands as to the Lord. For the husband is the head of the wife as Christ is the head of the church, his body, of which he is the Savior. Now as the church submits to Christ, so also wives should submit to their husbands in everything."

If that's all they read, it's easy to see how some people wrongly conclude that the Bible is actually promoting the idea that ours is a man's world, that everything in life should revolve around husbands, who are expected to take charge and always know what's best for us. Some critics have even mistakenly accused Promise Keepers of teaching this attitude because the organization encourages men to assume the spiritual leadership of the family.

Both misunderstandings could be easily corrected with a more careful look at what Paul was suggesting. The verse just prior to the passage we read undermines any such interpretation when it instructs men *and* women to: "Submit to one another out of reverence for Christ." And the later verses addressed directly to men—which immediately follow the instructions to women—also shed an entirely different light on marital relationships. Paul writes: "Husbands, love your wives, just as Christ loved the church and gave himself up for her." This isn't talking about a selfish, authoritarian type of dominance; Jesus lived an other-centered, sacrificial leadership model.

Both those professing Christians who want to use Scripture to bolster their own power agenda and those who would accuse Promise Keepers and other believers of promoting an outdated brand of repressive chauvinism have failed to understand one of the central tenets of Christianity and Jesus' teaching—the critical concept of servant leadership.

For as long as I've been a believer I've heard sermons on Ephesians 5:22–24 instructing women to submit to their husbands. But it wasn't until this past year, at a Promise Keepers conference, that I ever remember a sermon on verse 25—challenging men to demonstrate their love for their wives in the Christlike style of selfless sacrifice.

When I pointed this out to Randy, I asked him, "Why is that?" But it was a rhetorical question. We both knew the answer. True servant leadership is a difficult and revolutionary principle.

Until we all better understand what the Bible really says, a very basic issue of marriage will never be resolved. And more and more of you guys will be overlooking the sadness in your wives' eyes, scratching your heads, and wondering, *What does she mean when she says, "It's always been about you"?*

SO WHAT DOES SHE WANT FROM YOU, ANYWAY?

She wants you to:

- Acknowledge and allow for her feelings, her needs, her desires, and her dreams.
- Include her in your life and world.
- Think in terms of "we."
- Lead by serving.

chapter *4*

Why Is She Always Asking, "Honey, Do You Still Love Me?"

Reading the Signals You Give Her

Whenever I hear this question, I'm tempted to give the obvious, rather blunt answer: "She's probably asking the question because she's harboring some doubt about whether or not you *do* still love her. She just doesn't feel sure."

The trouble with such a straightforward response is that an awful lot of men have a difficult time taking the question at face value. Most of the men who wonder why their wives are asking, "Honey, do you still love me?" are honestly perplexed. They just can't believe their wives could be questioning their love: *Of course I love her! Isn't it obvious? How can she ever have any doubt? She has to know I love her!* So they figure they need to sift through complex layers of hidden meaning to figure out the underlying *real* question women are asking so they will know how to respond.

I'm here to tell you gentlemen, this *is* the real question. Contrary to the common assumption that it's somehow disguising a deeper issue, "Honey, do you still love me?" is itself the deeper, underlying question beneath countless other questions asked and comments made by your wives. Such as:

How do I look?

It's been a long time since the two of us had any time alone together.

Are you coming to bed soon?

You're working late again tonight?

Do you think you could turn off that ball-game so we can talk?

Remember when we were dating and we always _____? When was the last time we did that?

We never talk!

The unspoken, *real* question in any of these (and countless other) typical marriage scenarios could be, "Honey, do you still love me?" Indeed it may be the most common, most central, most underlying issue in our relationships. *Are we loved? Really? Truly? Still?*

This certainly was the essential question tormenting me on that fateful "night of the stoplights." For years in our marriage I'd been wondering and asking Randy in countless ways: "Do you love me anymore?" I'd eventually quit asking it because I was afraid I knew the answer. But that evening, when my counselor observed that Randy's responses in a number of situations hadn't seemed very loving, I knew I couldn't ignore this issue any longer. I needed to admit to myself and to my husband that I no longer believed I was loved.

SHOW-AND-TELL

So ... why is she always asking, "Honey, do you still love me?"

To answer this basic question, we need to first consider the ways love is conveyed. How do we convince someone we love her? Think about your own experience, your own relationship. When you have wanted to demonstrate or prove your love beyond a shadow of a doubt, how have you done it?

Ultimately all our expressions or demonstrations of love—no matter how creative, how dramatic, or how romantic—can be divided into two simple categories: Our *actions* and our *words*. It's as elementary as *show-and-tell*.

I want to examine the *words* part of the equation at some length in the next chapter. Here we're going to see and hear what our actions say. Do your actions speak louder than your words? Could she be fostering doubts and asking the question because what you *do* during the day communicates so much louder and clearer than what you whisper in bed at night?

Remember the story I told earlier about my fear of flying? How on that transcontinental flight to England Randy fell asleep and left me alone with my fear? As far as I was concerned, that was just one piece of proof I could later point to as evidence that Randy didn't love me anymore. There were others.

Perhaps the most painful, most hurtful of all the memories triggered on that night of the stoplights was an episode that took place approximately fifteen years into our marriage. It had happened the night before I was scheduled to check into Lutheran Hospital for back surgery. I'd struggled with a weak disc in my lower back for five years. I'd learned to live with pain. But after one fun-filled weekend tubing behind a boat on a nearby lake, the disc ruptured.

We'd put off the operation for as long as my doctor felt we could. But after two weeks of ice-packing and physical therapy, we had no choice. I was scared. I had never faced surgery before. So I was dreading the whole ordeal.

I went to bed with a major case of anxiety. After Randy fell asleep, it got even worse. Sometime after midnight the fear grew so intolerable that I became nauseous. I finally, gently, shook Randy awake.

"What's wrong?" he wanted to know, frustrated at being roused.

"I can't stop worrying about tomorrow," I confessed. "I feel like I'm about to be sick."

"It's going to be okay," Randy mumbled. "What you need most of all is a good night's sleep." With that he rolled over, pulled the covers up around his shoulders, and almost instantly dropped back off to sleep.

I knew I needed a good night's sleep. But how was I going to get it with this terror coursing through me? There I was, wide awake. Alone. More frightened than ever.

I desperately wanted to reawaken Randy and ask him to hold me. But by this time I was too embarrassed and hurt. Why couldn't he see and care that I was more terrified than I'd ever been in my life? His lack of compassion and easy sleep left me feeling hopelessly abandoned— humiliated by my own fear.

Finally, after watching my husband's peaceful, deep breathing, I felt I had no recourse but to slip out of bed. I made my way through the darkened house and down the stairs to the walk-in basement apartment where my mother lived. Quietly opening her bedroom door, I walked to the side of her bed and laid my hand softly on her shoulder.

She immediately awakened and sat up to ask, "What's the matter?"

I began to sob. "I'm sick and I'm scared, Mom," I managed to tell her. "Can I sleep with you?"

"Sure," she replied even as she moved over to make room. Mom took me in her arms, patting my back. For the rest of that long, horrible night, she stayed awake, doing everything she could to soothe and settle me.

When morning mercifully dawned, I stumbled back upstairs to get dressed and find a slow-stirring husband, who didn't seem to realize I'd been gone.

I was crushed. When I'd needed emotional support so desperately, my husband couldn't give it to me. And I hadn't even known how to ask him for it. Instead, like a little child, I'd had to go crying to my mother for help.

Randy went with me to the hospital that morning, of course. So he was *there* with me. But as the nurses wheeled me down the hall toward the operating room I felt so despondent, so dejected. I was silently confessing to God, *I really don't believe you love me enough to even want to wake me up from this surgery.* That was the last thing I remember thinking before the anesthesia took over.

Awakening in recovery a few hours later was something of a spiritual experience. The fact that I was alive, that I'd survived, I took as a sign. It seemed tangible reassurance that God did, in fact, love me.

But I was less than sure how Randy felt.

WHAT IS LOVE?

Why is she always asking, "Honey, do you still love me?"

If she's like me, the answer to this question probably overlaps the answer to the "Why is she so angry?" question. If she has been afraid or hurt sometime when you haven't been there for her—either physically or emotionally—she may be doubting your love. Your actions may be what is causing this fear. If you aren't tuned in to realize the problem, she may be convinced you don't love her anymore.

Let's consider what love is. A quick check of a thesaurus finds a few weak substitute nouns such as *passion, affinity, devotion, attraction,* and *warmth.* But as a verb we find many more telling synonyms such as *worship, esteem, adore, honor, value, cherish, treasure, respect,* and *regard.*

Perhaps the best, and certainly one of the most classic, definitions of love in all literature, can be found in 1 Corinthians 13: "Love is patient, love is kind. It does not envy, it does not boast, it is not proud. It is not rude, it is not self-seeking, it is not easily angered, it keeps no record of wrongs. Love does not delight in evil but rejoices with the truth. It always protects, always trusts, always hopes, always perseveres. Love never fails" (verses 4–8).

Love *in action* is clearly "other-centered." Any woman who feels, "It's always been about you" is going to have a hard time feeling very loved.

What compounds the problem is that even the most one-sided relationships probably didn't start out like that. They usually evolve over time. And the changes themselves raise questions and create doubts.

This can happen in the *best* of relationships. Chances are, it's happened in yours.

If you're not sure what I'm talking about, think back to your courting days. Remember the thrill you got just from being together? How you would look forward all day, or maybe all week, to the too-few and too-short hours when you could be in each other's company? Remember when you thought there was no mountain high enough, no ocean wide enough to keep you apart?

Randy and I met and would talk at a Bible study in downtown Honolulu. It was the one place, the one time of the week he knew where I'd be. So without fail, even if it meant hitchhiking in the rain, he'd find a way to get there. (And it wasn't because the teaching was all that great.)

Maybe when we're dating we get a distorted view of life. Perhaps romance isn't the most solid of foundations on which to build a lasting relationship. But most men seem to know, or they soon learn, that the best way to sweep a woman off her feet is to demonstrate their love by spending enormous amounts of time together, being attentive, thoughtful, considerate, and interested in every little detail of her life.

This is not insincere; no sacrifice seems too great to make when you're in love. And this is not all one-sided; women learn to do this, too. When the behavior of one or both people begins to change, feelings of doubt inevitably arise.

Remember when you could spend endless hours sitting together on a park bench or across a table from each other, gazing deeply into each other's eyes? When nothing in life seemed as important or as interesting as getting to know and understand everything about this fascinating person you were in love with?

When was the last time you spent looking into each other's eyes—trying to sense one another's heart and soul? When did you last spend any time trying to learn or understand something new about each other? Do you know all there is to know? Or just all you care to know?

What changed?

Life and its responsibilities change things. Circumstances change. Few of us have the time, let alone the inclination, to invest long hours making romantic moon-eyes at each other, talking endlessly about everything (and nothing), or just sitting and snuggling silently like we might have done early in our relationship.

Is love still there? Sometimes we can begin to have doubts. Love may be there, but without the familiar evidence and *actions* we associate with love, we simply don't get that "lovin' feelin'" anymore. We end up wondering, needing reassurance, and asking, "Do you still love me?"

We often ask it not so much because of some hurtful, unloving thing you *do*, but because of something you *don't* do. More specifically, some loving thing you don't do now that you used to do—back in the days when you could make us feel your world revolved around us and when we thought you'd hung the moon.

SPORTS WIDOWS

Could it be that at this point in your relationship, she doesn't feel you value her enough to even include her in your world—either your inner world of thoughts and feelings or your outer world of everyday experience? How might she come to that conclusion?

Anything that usurps our place, anything that bumps us off, or bumps us down your priority list, devalues us in the process. And whenever we're devalued, we feel unloved. Or at least less loved.

Does the term "golf widow" mean anything to you? I've known some. Every weekend their entire family's schedule is arranged around his tee time. Vacations become extended golf outings with travel destinations limited to locales offering the best golfing weather and the finest golf courses. Sometimes women are forced to take up the game themselves if they have any hope of spending time and reestablishing a relationship with their men.

I had a girlfriend tell me recently that for as long as she could remember, if she ever wanted time with her dad, it had to be on the course. On Mondays it was golf, Tuesdays it was couple's golf. Wednesdays more golf. Weekends he played tournaments (not professional, just friendly club competition). He never adjusted his golf schedule to accommodate his family. "If I hadn't learned how to play the game," she said, "I wouldn't even know my dad."

The same thing can happen with fishing, softball, automobile restoration, skiing, sailing, gardening, tinkering in the garage until all hours, collecting, woodworking, or any other pastime people enjoy. There's absolutely nothing wrong with these things. They are all fun, positive, beneficial activities. It's just that the time and energy expended in any such endeavors come from somewhere. Is it coming from time that could be spent with her? Or the kids?

I remember a time not that long ago when I felt the many demands on our lives—at work and at home—had been keeping Randy and me from spending enough time together. So I made a special point of letting my husband know of my desire to do something together on a regular basis—anything that would give me a chance to be with him and enjoy the pleasure of his company.

At least half a dozen times I mentioned how fun it would be to go biking like we did when we first dated. But even after he bought himself a new pair of cross-trainer shoes, and I bought him a mountain bike for his birthday, he still didn't invite me to go walking or riding with him. He walked by himself, and even took a bike trip with some of his friends—but did nothing with me.

The clear message I was getting was that my husband liked me so little that he would rather be anywhere than with me, and he'd walk or bike to get there!

Now you might be thinking, *A man needs his space—some time he can call his own.* And I agree. But we had talked. Randy knew I was all in favor of his going fishing alone or going on bike trips with his buddies. I'd even suggested he go on periodic retreats by himself—somewhere he didn't have to think about anyone else's needs.

But to hear him head out the door for a walk while I was busy fixing dinner or tending to other household responsibilities, or to see him riding his bike when I had one in the garage gathering dust, sent me the message that he didn't love me. While I now know it wasn't true—that he just didn't realize how serious I was about needing time together—I certainly *felt* unloved.

If your recreation and relaxation routinely take priority over marriage and family relationships, it can effectively shut your spouse out of a major part of your life. Is that what you want? When you routinely sacrifice time with your wife or kids, when she must regularly compete with some game or hobby for your attention, your interest, and your time, she's naturally going to begin wondering about your love for her.

Have the bulk of your family vacations been designed around golf, fishing, camping, or some other avocation you enjoy? Would you ever consider taking a holiday where she could shop till she drops, or you spent each night attending a different show (and I don't mean movies) and "getting cultured," or you planned a trip around some other interests she has? What would that say to her? Sound too radical?

Let me challenge you to administer an honest little self-assessment survey. Ask yourself: *What is it that consumes my time, my energy, and my money? What things in life am I most passionate about? What most excites, interests, and attracts me?* If she doesn't fit in there anywhere, chances are she already knows it. Could that be why she is always wondering if you still love her?

COMPETING WITH HIS CAREER

However, it's not hobbies, sports, and other optional electives in the curriculum of life that usually present the biggest competition for our marriages. Most often that challenge comes from the workplace.

It did for Randy and me. For years, my husband's work consumed so much of him, there never seemed to be much left for me or our family. Eventually we reached the point where I could no longer be satisfied with the leftovers.

Maybe the following observation has been distorted by my experience as a pastor's wife, but it seems to me that this scenario is most common in service occupations— careers that require working with and meeting the needs of other people.

If ministers aren't at the top of the list, they're close. So are doctors and anyone else who is almost always on call.

Sometimes it seems the higher, the nobler the sense of calling, the greater competition a spouse must feel.

But it can happen in any occupation, any job.

I can hear some of you guys saying, "Wait a minute! Work is good! My job isn't an option. What I do is important! Sure I work hard, but my career provides for the needs and security of my family. I'm working as much for them as for anyone else. Would she rather me be a deadbeat?"

You're right. No woman would prefer her husband to be irresponsible or neglectful.

Sometimes the problem is that we women misread the signals we're getting. We see how much of yourselves you are investing in work, how much time you are spending at the office, and we jump to the erroneous conclusion that you're tired of us and are running off to the office to avoid us. That's the way it feels.

Many times we fail to fully understand the sense of accomplishment and value men find in their work. We fail to recognize the pride men take in *providing* for the needs and security of those they love most.

At the same time, many of you men misunderstand something just as important to us women. You realize we need and appreciate a sense of security. But we need to be more appreciative of the hard work you invest in trying to provide us with security. We all need to understand that your idea of security and our idea of security may be two different things.

For most women, security isn't primarily a *material thing*. It doesn't come from knowing, in our heads, that all our needs are provided for. Security for women is primarily a *heart thing*. Our deepest feelings of security come from *feeling* loved and cared about.

We have a very difficult time feeling secure or loved when a job or a career becomes like "the other woman" in our husband's life. We resent it when he pours his best juices, devotes his prime time, and makes his highest commitment to "it" instead of the home front.

I've known and talked with countless women who feel they have to compete with their husbands' jobs. Some of these women have been deeply hurt by what they took as rejection. Others have been fearful they'll be left for "it." Many are frustrated and angry because "his job" has made her feel like a widow, or at least like a single mom, left to handle most of the family and child-raising responsibilities on her own. More than a few have gradually grown cold because they've burned themselves out trying to make him understand their hurt, their fear, their frustration, and their bitterness. So why try anymore?

Lyndi McCartney knew that sense of despair. In Bill McCartney's autobiography, *From Ashes to Glory*, Lyndi says:

> There were enormous penalties that came with [Bill's] success. Everybody wanted a piece of Bill, and he kept giving it to them. I resented it deeply. It wasn't that the things he was doing were bad. They were very good and marvelous. It was just that he couldn't find time to say yes to me.
>
> I spent about a year in isolation. The kids were out and on their own. So it was just the two of us in the house. I didn't answer the telephone, and I shut the door on all outsiders. I even shut out friends who loved me. I thought I needed time to myself. I realized we had run amuck, and even though thirty years together had generated many great, loving memories, I had to confront my own bitterness.
>
> I was hopelessly caught, eyebrow deep, in pain. And I was blind to all the good. I was a wounded, ugly woman.
>
> I read more than a hundred books in 1993. I read book after book on recovery, on healing, and on restoration. More importantly, I read the Bible constantly. I practically ate books—in fact, I ate little else.

I lost seventy pounds that year—thirty of them in January alone. It was a very scary time. I was totally and completely withdrawn.

I had kept things inside for so long. I didn't let Bill see my pain.

When it finally all came gushing out, I'm sure he was surprised—even shocked—at some of the things I had to say. I told him I needed to be on his calendar. So he began penciling me in. But then I got erased a couple of times. So I went back and told him I wanted to be written in ink.

"It's ink or nothing," I told him. I think he got the message.

Ink or nothing! Those words of Lyndi McCartney capture the sentiments of a lot of women I know. I know they captured mine. In fact, Randy and I just got finished doing our calendar for next year, and the first thing he put in ink was our date night every week and second was our family time. To him they are now nonnegotiable.

CONSIDER THESE QUESTIONS

Why is she always asking, "Honey, do you still love me?"
Could it be that she's been penciled in and erased too many times? Could it be that your commitment to your job sometimes seems greater than your commitment to her?

If this is the case in your life, if you have invested the best of yourself in your job, if you find your primary identity in the work you do, try asking yourself these questions:

Does the title "husband" or "father" seem as important a part of your identity as your title or job description at work? What would happen if you allowed your wife and family to become the fuel that lights your fire? What message are you communicating when you come home so late night after night? Why don't you want to come home? Has your home, your family, your marriage, your wife become so less attractive to you? Does your wife feel discouraged, lonely, and abandoned because she's lost the best part of you to your work?

It may be time for you to do what Bill McCartney did when he looked into Lyndi's eyes and finally noticed her sadness. It may be time for you to recognize your responsibility. To realize your overcommitment to your work may explain why she is always asking, "Honey, do you still love me?"

SO WHAT DOES SHE WANT FROM YOU, ANYWAY?

She wants you to:

- Show that you love her by what you do.
- Do something she wants instead of what you want.
- Use ink on your schedule for her. Use pencil for everything else.
- Consider the hours spent at work. Are they necessary and reasonable?

chapter **5**

What Am I Supposed to Say?
Solving the Mystery of How,
When, and What to Communicate

Not long ago Promise Keepers received a poignant letter from a man who admitted he was really struggling in his relationships. He wanted the Promise Keepers staff to be praying for him and for his wife. He wrote:

"The area I have the most trouble with is in expressing my feelings. I usually stuff them inside. I never feel too comfortable sharing with others one-to-one.

"For instance, just my doing business day-to-day involves communication. But I do my best to initiate as little contact as possible. I have the biggest problem letting people know my *needs*. And when I do, I usually feel shame.

"I have had many dreams and plans for my business and my life. But when I try to talk about them, a gush of self-doubt hits me, and I end up throwing the plan away or filing it in the back of some drawer and trying to forget about it.

"The other sad part is when I get down on myself like this, I won't let anyone else into my world. I push my wife and kids away and feel even more frustrated. We hardly know each other.

"I want to ask for help. But instead I freeze up, and then I get more discouraged."

Recently I read the words of another man who acknowledged his struggles in communicating. In a magazine article intended to help women better understand men (*Today's Christian Woman*, July/August 1995), James Charis wrote:

> "Is something bothering you?" my wife, Elaine, asked as I absentmindedly channel-surfed.
>
> "Nope," I replied as I continued to click the TV remote.
>
> "Are you sure? You look kind of down," she persisted.
>
> "Nothing's bothering me. Okay?"
>
> "Okay."
>
> Wait a minute! My wife left out something. She's supposed to say, "Okay, but if something is bothering you, I'll be glad to listen."
>
> And then, I'm supposed to answer, "Well ... (dramatic pause) ... well, there is this one thing ..."
>
> At least that's how the scene played out from kindergarten through community college in my biological family. I would be upset. My mother would persist in her questioning. Until, finally, I would tell her what was wrong.
>
> Unfortunately I carried that well-worn script into my marriage. My wife never got a copy. And so, many times in our early years together, I never expressed what I was really feeling.
>
> Deep inside, I wanted to tell my wife what kind of day I really had at the office, what I really felt when she seemed unsatisfied during our lovemaking, and what I really feared about turning forty. But more times than

not, such sharing was cut short with the click of the TV remote and a quick "Nothing's bothering me."

I continue to be amazed—and maybe a bit envious—that two women can meet as total strangers and within five minutes be discussing their feelings! Somehow, we guys don't often get past, "What do you do for a living?"

Two guys with two different stories, both struggling with communication. They remind us that for a variety of reasons many men are asking, in one form or another, the question: *What am I supposed to say? What does she want me to talk about? Why is it so important that we talk?*

In the previous chapter I made the point that ultimately all our expressions or demonstrations of love—no matter how creative, how dramatic, or how romantic—can be divided into two simple categories: actions and words. Both are forms of communication.

We've seen what our actions can communicate. I think what we say and how we say it can be just as important.

Most guys I know are more comfortable showing than telling. Given a choice they'd pick *actions* over *words*. They'd rather *do* something than *talk* about almost anything.

And yet more and more men concerned about their relationships are searching for help. They hear conference speakers, counselors, and other experts laud the benefits of improved verbal communication. Every book about marriage contains at least one chapter on the subject; many books are exclusively dedicated to the topic. And all the experts preach the same message: Verbal communication is critically important to relationships. Men are told again and again that they are going to have to talk if they want their relationships to go forward.

Many men have also learned that *not* communicating sends a message of its own. We intuitive women are practiced at reading the smallest nuances in nonverbal communication. If nothing is said, we're very good at jumping to our own conclusions. If you're not talking, we may conclude that you don't want to talk, that you don't care, or that you don't love us anymore.

Most couples experience this, which helps explain the sense of urgency I often hear behind men's question: *What am I supposed to say?*

To answer that question, we need to identify some common barriers that arise when we try to communicate. We need to honestly address this related question: Why don't men and women—particularly husbands and wives—communicate better?

There's no one simple answer. In fact, there are a ton of reasons, many of which overlap and interact to complicate the issue. And the first big reason we don't communicate better is this:

Men and women are different.

This seems obvious. In our enlightened age, this statement is not politically correct; however, it is true. And the truth is seldom more evident than in communication.

I don't want to sound sexist or stereotypical when I say this, but my own experience has convinced me that, in general, women are simply more verbal than men. Conversation seems like their natural element. Indeed, most women take to words like fish to water.

In contrast, most men feel like they are in danger of drowning in a bottomless ocean of words. They may gingerly test the waters of communication by wading slowly into safe and shallow conversations. But they're always uneasy, knowing if the tides of communication suddenly shift, they can be in over their heads (or at least over their hearts) in no time.

Why do men and women seem so different on this score? Some people think the reason lies in our basic biological inheritance—that it has everything to do with the differences in genetic wiring in those X and Y chromosomes. Other folks seem just as convinced the differences are learned—that men and women communicate differently because we've been conditioned by our upbringing and our exposure to the world around us.

What we're talking about here is a variation on the age-old "nature versus nurture" debate. So we could argue the two sides till the end of time. Let's not.

Knowing the answer isn't nearly as important as acknowledging differences do exist. And understanding those differences helps explain why we don't communicate better.

Why can't we just accept that, as noted author and speaker Gary Smalley says, *Men need ten thousand words and women need twenty-five thousand words a day in order to feel they have communicated.* Is it so important to know why? Can't we just accept that these things seem to be inherent? It's proven out daily. Why not just respect and appreciate the differences and not place unfair expectations on each other?

Here's another reason we don't communicate better:

Men tend to isolate and internalize.

John Gray illustrates this point in *Men Are from Mars, Women Are from Venus* with his analogy of modern males as emotional cave dwellers. He's not slandering guys as primitive Neanderthals; he's using imagery to help readers picture what he sees as the common masculine behavior pattern of retreating into the far recesses of their daily lives to process emotions—in private and alone.

The letter I quoted at the beginning of this chapter is an extreme example of this very thing—of retreating, isolating, and internalizing. Most men do it to a greater or lesser degree. Randy internalizes, and always has, since before we were married.

When Randy and I met, he was a Private First Class stationed at an Army base in Hawaii where my Lt. Colonel father was also assigned. Parking spots were at a premium on base, and where you parked was determined by special base registration. Randy received a new assignment on base and, for some reason or other, didn't get around to updating his registration so he could legally park near his office. So the MPs ticketed his car. Randy stuck the ticket in his glove compartment and forgot about it. But before he could get his registration updated, he received another ticket, which he also stuck in his glove compartment.

Before he realized it, Randy had accumulated such a batch of citations that the MPs began staking out his car to catch the culprit. Randy managed to evade them, but realized if he registered now, he could be in big trouble.

A few weeks before our scheduled wedding I sensed something was wrong. By this time Randy was not only worried about getting caught and severely disciplined, he was embarrassed that he'd let things go this far. He worried what my dad would think (being an officer and all). He was afraid to tell me because he thought he'd lose my respect. He was ashamed.

It took some coaxing on my part before Randy finally opened up. When he did, I think I surprised him with concern and empathy. And when I encouraged him to face the music, the support gave him the gumption to go to his commanding officer and admit what he'd done. Incredibly, his CO simply took all of his citations, tossed them in the wastebasket, and said, "Don't worry about it. I'll take care of it."

What a relief that was for both of us! And what a lesson for Randy, who saw that I loved him no matter what he'd done. Far from losing my respect, he'd actually endeared himself to me by opening up and allowing me to share his private distress.

While I do think Randy saw the benefits of openly and honestly communicating his most pressing emotions, I can't claim that it was a once-and-for-all lesson. Throughout our marriage we've *both* struggled to break the comfortable pattern of isolation and internalization. And truthfully, for several years in the second decade of our marriage, before I was able to drop the anger and bitterness I was harboring, I adopted the same retreating behavior. I didn't want to communicate anymore. I was withdrawn. Why? Hurt and apathy.

This pattern is hard for anyone to break out of, but perhaps hardest of all for men. As James Charis was trying to explain to women in the magazine article I quoted earlier, most men want to express their emotions . . .

> . . . [But] for most of our lives, men have been told, "Big boys don't cry," "Sticks and stones may break your bones, but words will never hurt you," and "Be a man!" (which translated means, "Don't show emotions!"). And so, even though we feel like crying and words do hurt, we inflict an emotional lobotomy on ourselves.
>
> Instead of shedding tears, men secrete stomach acid.

Charis goes on to confess:

> When I would "lose it" while speaking at various conferences and tears would begin to form, I feared losing the respect of men in the audience. I'd quickly joke, "I'm not crying. My head's just leaking." But I discovered men want to be able to express emotion. One conferee admitted, "I admire your ability to expose yourself in public." He quickly clarified, "That's not exactly what I mean! You know, it's just we'd probably be healthier if we could be more honest about our feelings."

My conversations with men have convinced me that many are beginning to believe this, but are finding it tough to break the old habits of emotional withdrawal and retreat.

Men and women see and use conversation differently.

This is probably the biggest reason we don't do a better job of communicating.

You guys deal with problems by identifying them and then moving directly to the solution. We women typically want to discuss the problem until we feel satisfied it, and all our feelings about it, have been adequately acknowledged and understood. But when we approach you with this intent, you feel like an avalanche of issues and emotions have flooded and overtaken you. If you try to move straight to the solution once the problem has been identified, we feel the real issue is being lost and our feelings are being completely disregarded. My friend John Maxwell likes to say, "People don't care how much you know, until they know how much you care." That is certainly true of women when it comes to communicating with men.

In other words, for women, *talking* about something shows caring and is an important problem-solving technique—it's often how we think and process information. Talking is an end in itself. For you men, talking is simply a means of identifying the problem. And it's something you *might* do at the end of the thinking and deciding process.

Yet another reason why men and women don't communicate better is because ...

Men often don't feel like they are good at it.

If this seems a tad redundant, bear with me. The point is important.

It's human nature for us to enjoy what we do well and do well what we enjoy. And because we don't enjoy what we're not naturally good at, we may actually avoid those things. This is true in most jobs. Think about it—the part of our job description we are best at is almost always the part we really enjoy.

Tom Landry, the legendary Dallas Cowboys football coach who has spoken at some of our Promise Keeper events, made a very pertinent point in his autobiography about achieving success:

> Too many teams contentedly spend their practices working on the areas in which they are already good. Everyone likes to do that. It's easier and more immediately satisfying. But if you want a football team to improve, you need to identify the areas in which you aren't as good and practice those. Then you'll have a shot at [success].

The same dynamics apply to relationships. The parts of the relationship game we feel we're best at, we want to practice the most. Those areas where we're naturally weaker (for men it's often communication), we avoid. As a result, we'll get even weaker in those areas over time and lose our best shot at success.

Men are naturally protective.

What can this possibly have to do with why men and women don't communicate better?

Again, we could spend all day fruitlessly arguing what is inherited and what is learned. But whether or not it's God-given nature or merely behavior passed down through generations of men since the days of primitive warrior cultures, most men almost instinctively assume a defensive, protector role when they sense any danger or threat.

And for the reasons we've already talked about, communication can seem threatening to many men.

Emotionally honest, open conversation can make a man feel vulnerable. What he shares may come back to haunt him. It may be used against him. He may find it hard to handle her emotional reaction. A good warrior isn't going to expose himself to that unnecessary risk.

But neither does a warrior want to expose those he loves. So there are times when guys are reluctant to communicate something that might in any way upset or hurt their wives.

Randy is like this. When he's distressed about something, his natural tendency is to keep quiet about it, because he's afraid it will distress me, or because he's embarrassed and doesn't want to be weak in front of his wife. That's what was going on with the tickets in the glove compartment before we got married. And with other incidents since.

Sometimes this natural desire to protect a spouse from being hurt is not such a good idea. Some things, some very difficult things, she may need to know. But that "protector" mind-set prevents the necessary communication from taking place.

Men may be harboring deep, dark secrets that are taking a serious toll.

It's impossible to build a wall high enough to seal off some particularly painful, unresolved secret issue (whether it's homosexuality, an affair, or addiction to pornography, drugs, or alcohol) without destroying or damaging the entire communication process and therefore the overall relationship.

One husband I know struggled with latent homosexual tendencies for years, but could never open up and tell his wife because he knew how hurtful it would be for her. He tried to keep any evidence of his personal battle buried deep inside.

Eventually temptation got the better of him, and some years ago, he fell into an adulterous homosexual affair. The strain of secrecy grew even heavier—casting a dark shadow over every aspect of their relationship. She sensed something was wrong, but she didn't find out what the problem was until the affair was publicly exposed. It was the most devastating blow in her life. He lost his job. They were ostracized by their community, and she was emotionally crushed.

Even though he repented and turned his life around, years passed before they could overcome the stigma of his indiscretion. Amazingly this couple is still together. She wholeheartedly loves and supports him. God took the shipwreck of their marriage and set it afloat again.

But I can't help wondering how much easier God's job would have been, how much pain might have been avoided, if they'd been able to communicate before disaster struck. I'm convinced she would have loved and supported him through his early struggles—because that's how she responded in the end. But she never had the chance because, for so long, the issues he struggled with seemed too much to talk about.

Incidentally, women aren't the only ones who suffer sexual mistreatment as children. This man was a victim of sexual abuse at the hands of a man when he was a young boy. Then again as a teenager he was abused by someone from whom he could not defend himself. While I suspect those incidents played a role in his acting out in his adult life, these too were secrets he couldn't admit to his wife until after the worst of the damage had been done.

A lot of men honestly don't know *what* to communicate.

When guys ask me, *What I am supposed to say?* they are not simply wondering what words to use. Many of them don't even have a clue where to start. Even some very involved husbands and fathers, who spend a commendable amount of time talking with their wives about the kids and the business of family living, seldom seem to communicate about anything deeper than the surface details of their day-to-day lives.

As important and necessary as it is to touch base regularly on the nitty-gritty details of our daily existence, real relationships require more than that. So for those of you who don't have a clue what else you should be communicating, and for all the rest of us who need periodic reminding, I'd like to suggest a cheat sheet—a checklist of talking points that could be a regular part of our communication. I hope these few guidelines will get the discussion started.

The first three things that need to be communicated are all closely related and focused on your spouse: *Praise, appreciation,* and *value.* When we express the first two, we bestow the last one. And we've already seen the importance of feeling valued in a relationship.

While I was working on this book, a friend of mine shared a story that illustrates what we're talking about here.

A couple of years ago this friend helped his wife throw a birthday party for their six-year-old son. For two hours a horde of kindergartners invaded their home and yard. While he enjoyed his son's excitement, my friend admitted, "I was ready to end the celebration long before those other kids' parents returned to pick them up. My wife, on the other hand, never seemed to wear down. She was truly amazing. For two solid hours she managed that mini-mob—drawing out the shy ones, directing games, distributing prizes, and serving refreshments—all the while watching to make sure every child was having a good time.

"When the last visitor had driven off with his parents, I told my wife, 'You sure throw a great party. I really appreciate all the special things you do for our kids. You're a wonderful mother!'

"'Thanks,' my wife reacted in surprise. 'I need to hear that more often.'

"I felt challenged by my wife's response. She has to be one of the most creative, loving, dedicated, and selfless mothers in the world. But I couldn't remember the last time I told her that. It hurt to think she was surprised by my praise and had to remind me that she needed to hear my affirmation more often.

"I vowed that afternoon to do a lot better job of appreciating my wife and letting her know it. But I have to admit I still fail much of the time. I don't know why it's so hard. It just doesn't come naturally."

Praise, appreciation, and value. If these three words were regular features in our communication, they might eventually seem more natural.

What else needs to be communicated? Now shifting focus to self-expression, I'd suggest three more words with an acronym any American male can remember: N-F-L.

N for *needs*. I know it isn't very macho for you to admit you need someone else—particularly a woman. And with the advent of feminism it's no longer considered appropriate for us women to admit we need men either. But even so, it is very human. Surely we're not too proud to admit we all have needs. And we all need to be needed.

So look for ways she might be able to assist you. And ask her for help.

I will never forget the day a few years ago now when Randy did this for me. I knew Promise Keepers had been contacted by a major Christian record label to produce an album with a sampling of music from our conferences. But I was shocked when Randy told me he needed me to be PK's liaison to work with the recording company.

"But I'm not a businessperson," I protested. "I've never negotiated or done anything like this before."

What Does She *Want* from Me, Anyway?

"No one else on staff knows the music like you do," Randy insisted. "You can learn the rest. You've got what it takes to do this, Holly. You can do the job. You've got a lot to offer here. And I know I can trust you."

I remember feeling so overwhelmed. Randy's needing me made me feel incredibly valued. His request for my help made me feel so affirmed that it began to revolutionize our relationship.

F is for *feelings.* We've already talked about how hard it is for many guys to articulate their emotions. Males have the same basic feelings females have. You guys aren't so much emotionally challenged as you are verbally challenged—at least when it comes to putting your deepest feelings into words.

But I want to encourage you by promising, *If you'll try, she'll love you all the more for it.* She needs to know all your feelings—even if those feelings are negative. And even if some of them are aimed at her.

Are you angry at her? She needs to know. In an unaccusing tone, in a peaceful environment, at an unemotional time. Chances are she's already picked up the indications on her radar and is jumping to conclusions. She may be reading your anger as a lack of love.

You're a human being; you have the right to express your feelings even when the truth of those feelings may be painful. (We can talk later about how to do that effectively.) Communication is not a one-sided privilege. You shouldn't steer away from it simply because you feel threatened by the possible repercussions.

L is for *love.* You can communicate love indirectly by doing and saying a lot of the things we've already talked about. But I think we'd all agree love needs to be articulated, too.

Remember the old joke about the woman pressing her unexpressive husband for verbal assurance of his continued affection? He responds in exasperation: "I told you I

116

loved you when I asked you to marry me! If that ever changes, I'll let you know!"

The reason that's become such an old joke is that it's merely an exaggeration of an all-too-familiar attitude. And I suspect a lot of women laugh in order to keep from crying, because it rings all too true.

Why don't we communicate better? If you honestly don't know *what* to communicate, I'd challenge you to remember six simple words: praise, appreciation, value, needs, feelings, love (NFL). Communicate those, and you'll revolutionize any relationship.

There's one more answer I want to give to those of you who may be asking the question: *What am I supposed to say?*

Sometimes you don't have to say anything at all.

I can practically hear some of you responding, "All right! No problem! I'm good at that!" Which is why I saved this answer for last. I first wanted you to understand how all the other factors we've talked about affect your communication. But sometimes our relationships as well as our communication can be enhanced by what we *don't* say.

Randy and I have had to learn this the hard way. On more occasions than I care to count, Randy has reached a point where he was finally willing to let down his defenses and disclose things gnawing at his insides. No sooner has he begun to share something he's been struggling with— a sense of failure, fear about the future, anger toward someone who has wronged him—than I butt in. Before he has a chance to get it all out, I'm overwhelming him with my own feelings about his feelings, trying to reassure him, or jumping to his defense and getting ready to take on whatever person has offended my man.

That isn't what he needed or wanted at all. He needed me to just be quiet and listen, to give him opportunity to vent. He was weighted down enough with his own feelings; he couldn't handle all the issues I added to the load.

It took me years to learn that my hair-trigger response was shutting Randy up. He was counting the cost three and four times before he opened up, because he didn't know if he could deal with my reactions on top of everything else.

I understand and recognize this problem now. But I confess it's still very hard to be quiet, because I'm such a ready communicator. And natural-born communicators have a hard time knowing when to keep still and quiet.

Many men have their own problem sitting back and just listening. Not because they feel driven to get their own two cents worth in, but because a man's natural tendency is to immediately *do* something to solve the problem. Most men are instinctively "fixers." They listen only long enough to identify what they think the problem is and then start proposing solutions. And that response is as apt to frustrate a woman as my response is to shut Randy up. So we all have some important lessons we need to learn about listening.

Some years ago now, behavioral scientists conducted some very telling research. They designed a rather simple experiment to measure people's ability to interpret non-verbal communication. First, they photographed faces registering a range of common human emotional reactions. Then they asked subjects to identify the emotions with no other clues than the close-up photos of strangers' faces.

The subjects did remarkably well identifying and distinguishing between reactions such as fear, anger, surprise, happiness, pain, sorrow, and so on. The photo that invariably gave people the most trouble showed the face of a person listening intently. "Listening intently" was most often misidentified as "unconditional love."

What does that tell us?

SEX AND COMMUNICATION

I have one last thing to bring up on this subject of communication—which leads very nicely into the question asked in the upcoming chapter: "Why Does Sex Have to Be Such a Touchy Subject?" (Pun intended.)

The whole idea of being intimate involves openness, vulnerability, risk taking. Isn't that what you expect and want from your wife in the marriage bed?

I'd like to propose a trade here. Her openness, vulnerability, risk taking, and all-embracing acceptance of you in the marriage bed for your openness, vulnerability, risk taking, and emotional disclosure in conversation and communication.

How about it? Is that a deal you could live with?

I imagine some of you guys are saying "Yeah, baby!" If so, you're probably more than ready for our next chapter.

SO WHAT DOES SHE WANT FROM YOU, ANYWAY?

She wants you to:

- Know that your honor skyrockets when you share openly. So let her know your needs. Be honest with your struggles, fears, doubts, and concerns. She wants to be a part of them.
- Understand and appreciate the real difference between men and women . . . especially where communication is involved.
- Realize she doesn't care how much you know until she knows how much you care.
- Work on the areas you feel you're the weakest.
- Listen.
- Become an MVP in the NFL.

chapter **6**

Why Does Sex Have to Be Such a Touchy Subject?

Revealing Reasons She May Not Respond the Way You Expect

How would you feel if someone asked you to go on live national television to discuss this question candidly? If you get a queasy feeling in the pit of your stomach and think *No way!* then you have a pretty good idea how I felt about tackling this chapter.

At one point in the writing of this book I said, "I don't think I can do it. I can't be that vulnerable. We just won't have a chapter on sex."

But everybody I talked to said the same thing: "You can't write a book about the biggest questions men have about their relationships without saying something about sex. It's just too important an issue to ignore." They merely confirmed what I knew was true.

So here we are.

Before we go any farther I want to make it very clear that I am not an expert on sexual relationships. I'm not a counselor with file cabinets full of case folders and clients' stories to draw from. I'm your average, red-blooded, middle-aged American woman. Most of the insights I offer have been gained from my own personal experience and from that of a fairly small number of women and men with whom I've felt free to discuss this topic.

I've concluded that just as many women as men are asking, "Why does sex have to be such a touchy subject?" But since this book is aimed at guys (and two of my goals are to encourage men and help them better understand the underlying issues of their relationships), I'm going to limit our discussion. All I intend to do here is suggest several possible reasons why we women may not always respond sexually in the way you expect or wish we would.

Other factors may be at play in your relationship. After all, human sexuality is as incredibly complex as it is wonderful. Yet I feel confident that one or more of the issues we raise here will be pertinent to you or to your spouse.

SEXUAL ATTITUDE

The first reason sex is such a touchy subject may be that one or both of you came into the relationship with a faulty, perhaps even destructive, attitude toward sex.

For example, many women walk into marriage with the attitude that men are animals when it comes to sex. I have heard women communicate this time and again over the course of years. And that stereotype was reinforced for me by the early experiences I had.

It wasn't until several years into marriage that I read a very helpful book called *The Act of Marriage* (by Tim and Beverly LaHaye), from which I gained an insight I think more women need. I finally began to understand that God made men with an intense, natural drive that is not only emotional, but also physical in a way different from a woman's sex drive. If more women not only understood, but truly appreciated this divinely designed difference, they might be more understanding of their men. You men wouldn't be made to feel so guilty for the strength of your God-given desires. And it would be easier for us women to be more responsive when you express them.

So a lot of women need to change their attitudes toward sex.

But so do many men.

One reason you've gotten the "Men are animals" rap is that it is animal-like to be sexually aggressive, noncaring, insistent, forceful, and demanding without regard for the dignity or the feelings of your mate. Too many men look at their wives and think, *Your body is mine.* But that's not a servant's attitude. It's a gimme-gimme, take-take attitude.

And it's wrong!

Some men with this attitude try to justify themselves biblically by using that same quote from Ephesians we talked about earlier where Paul wrote, "Wives, submit to your husbands as to the Lord ..." And once again they ignore the balancing verse that comes right before it which says: "Submit to one another ..." Another place Paul instructs us to "prefer one another" in love (Romans 12:10).

He's saying we each need to be thinking of the other person first, instead of thinking of ourselves first. That means setting my preference aside and regarding a spouse's feelings as more important than mine.

That's a far cry from the selfish attitude many men and women have toward sex, which may be a big part of the problems between us in this important area of our relationship.

SEXUAL HISTORY

Another reason sex is such a touchy subject may be the sexual history one partner or the other (or both) brings into a relationship.

Every child is created with a need to be loved, nurtured, held, and cared about. I was so starved for all of those things that by the time I was eight I had begun to look for love in all the wrong places. And this set me up for a world of hurt. In those days I would have sold my soul for a morsel of attention or acceptance, and I ended up doing just that. I was taken advantage of, used, and tossed aside.

At the age of seventeen, I had a blinding crush on a young guy. He used my fear of disapproval and rejection as an opportunity to take me to a place where he could "force the issue." That one incident forever changed my life.

When I became a Christian in my late teens, shortly before I met Randy, my life dramatically turned around. It truly was as if I were reborn. I broke off unhealthy relationships. I walked away from the past and into a fresh new start. I latched onto that verse the apostle Paul wrote describing conversion: "Old things are passed away; behold, all things are become new" (2 Corinthians 5:17 KJV). I figured I'd buried the pain and ugliness of my past for good. And it was a wonderful, freeing feeling.

My relationship with Randy was unlike any other I'd ever had. The two of us became friends before I began to fall in love. When romance blossomed, we determined to wait until marriage before we consummated our relationship. A short engagement proved an essential part of this successful strategy!

In the fresh excitement of our honeymoon years, I really did think I had dealt with my past. I had buried and forgotten it. Randy and I were so in love I didn't think history could come back to haunt us. But it did.

When other problems arose—issues we've already talked about, such as anger, feeling devalued and unloved, feeling like I was just an accessory to Randy's career, communication difficulties—the old wounds from a sexual past were quickly opened, and they oozed their poison into our marriage relationship.

Though I didn't recognize the source of the problem for a long time, the damage done was typical of those with my history. At times I desperately wanted the assurance of my husband's love and affection, and yet part of me was afraid to let him get too close. I'd been "used" in the past, so I couldn't totally trust Randy's motives. I could never feel absolutely certain that he really loved me and wasn't just doing what he had to do to get what he really wanted from me.

Gentlemen, all of us are born with a need for love. This hunger for love can be the driving reason so many women are willing to sell themselves short and compromise their principles to make their men happy. Even women who have not endured the trauma of sexual violation may suffer from some of the same effects if they have engaged in premarital sex.

When a woman falls in love and gives herself completely to a man for the first time, she makes herself vulnerable. She usually believes that this is the one true love of her life. If that relationship falls apart, she then feels betrayed and rejected. She has shown him the most intimate part of herself and has been found lacking.

In her next relationship, intimacy is more likely to occur sooner. This is because she is searching for someone who will treasure and value that most personal part of her, not just for the moment, but for a lifetime. Each time she gives herself to a man who then walks away, she loses a part of herself, underscoring the feeling, *Something must be very wrong with me. I must not be worthy of love.* (Where did we ever get the idea that engaging in a physical act was equal to love?)

People—men and women alike—with a premarital history walk into marriage carrying baggage. Sometimes they've lost such an important part of themselves their self-esteem is seriously scarred. Or the memories of those old encounters linger like unwanted ghosts persistently haunting their relationships. They may well expect no promise for commitment, an agenda calling for personal gratification, and no hope for give-and-take. Such expectations rob us of emotional intimacy, freedom in the marriage bed, and the potential for an honest and open friendship with our spouse. The joy of sex sadly becomes intertwined with pain, loss, fear, and self-doubt.

Our sexual pasts do have an effect on our present and future.

SEXUAL ABUSE

If either of you has experienced sexual abuse, raising this subject will stir up painful memories that could take much emotional energy and a lot of time to work through. You may well need to get professional help to assist you through the process. If you attempt to ignore this issue, it can metastasize and spread beyond your sexual relationship until it affects your entire relationship and outlook on life. I know because this happened with Randy and me.

My history not only undermined my relationship with Randy, it warped my view of myself. Even before anyone else ever suspected, before I admitted it to myself, I knew a deep and secret shame that made me feel terribly unlovable.

One night ten years into our marriage, Randy was gone for the evening, so I flipped on some made-for-TV movie. I'd been watching for a few minutes, trying to catch up on the plot, when suddenly, without warning, there appeared on the screen a scene of a young girl being raped. That visual image, in an instant, managed to crack a barrier I'd constructed deep in my soul. I quickly shut off the TV. But the damage had been done. An overwhelming flood of memory and pain from my life of long ago gushed through my mind. When Randy returned home later that night, I was huddled in bed, still sobbing uncontrollably.

"What happened? What's wrong?" he wanted to know.

Between sobs I managed what I suspect was only a semicoherent explanation of what I'd seen. Then I admitted to my husband the painful memories I'd tried to block out of my conscious mind for so many years.

Like most people who have been sexually mistreated (particularly as children), I couldn't shake the irrational feeling that the entire thing had somehow been my fault. So even though Randy listened and held me and was lovingly supportive as I poured out my pain, what I remember most vividly about that evening was my own consuming sense of humiliation and shame. Those feelings of self-condemnation echoed through my life and marriage for years.

My unresponsiveness was never a rejection of Randy. It wasn't that I didn't want to be with him. It's just that I had all these memory tapes replaying in my mind.

Because of my history, sex seemed like a two-sided coin. At the same time I wanted to embrace it as an expression of love, another part of me was thinking, *It's only an act*—just something to fulfill him personally.

I've always had to fight that lie to believe what I now know is the truth. The dearest, most precious way my husband can show me that he loves me is in the intimacy of the marriage bed. It's taken me a long, long time to finally believe that. Even today, when Randy says, "Holly, I love you. I want us to be close," I sometimes catch myself wondering, *Does he really mean that? Or does he have an ulterior motive?*

Anyone's earliest exposure to sex has such a lasting impact!

At one of the Promise Keepers conferences, a woman volunteer who'd heard my words to the men stopped me in a stadium corridor to ask if there was somewhere we could talk. We found an out-of-the-way corner, and she told me her story. This middle-aged woman told me about being raised by a mother who was a prostitute. She said her childhood years exposed her to things no child should ever have to see. She witnessed so much ugliness and perversion that when she finally got old enough to escape that environment and take control of her own life, she vowed never to let anything like that happen to her or anyone she cared about ever again. While that determination seemed admirable, she admitted that her experience had made her a terribly controlling person. This expressed itself in several ways. She became an obsessively clean and neat housekeeper. And, without meaning to, she had become just as controlling of her husband and children. She was so protective of the kids, so worried about protecting them from the things she saw as a child, that she seldom allowed them to go anywhere and even severely restricted their television viewing. Her kids and husband saw her as an unbearable nag. "My kids are rebelling, and I'm afraid my husband is going to leave because he doesn't know what to do with me," she said, wiping away a tear that ran out from behind her sunglasses. "They don't understand the history that's driving my obsession and crippling our family life."

Many men *do* understand the shame and the pain resulting from inappropriate exposure to or experience with sex early in life. Women aren't the only ones who have been abused.

And this is one more reason we need to talk honestly. One more area in which to be open with each other. One more opportunity to "prefer one another" in love.

PORNOGRAPHY

A common problem is an exposure (past or present) to pornography. Pornography impacted my life in at least two significant ways. The sexually explicit material I saw in my childhood reinforced my unhealthy attitude: when it came to sex, women were objects that existed for the gratification and pleasure of men. In demeaning women, pornography also demeaned me.

Pornography spawned a whole pattern of inappropriate behavior of which I became a target as a girl. When I hear people argue that pornography is harmless, I want to scream out in protest. Because, without a shadow of a doubt, it was the by-product of pornography that robbed me of my childhood innocence and had serious ramifications on my life and my marriage.

You may think me a bit fanatical on this subject, but I don't think most men begin to realize the pain commonly felt by a woman whose husband routinely enjoys flipping through *Playboy*, or even less explicit publications such as lingerie catalogs. On some level she wonders, "What's wrong with me? Am I not enough for him?" She suddenly feels as if she's in competition with the airbrushed beauty of the women in those pictures. And since it's a competition she can't win, she ends up feeling demeaned.

The second concern I have about such publications in the home is the danger they present for the next generation. Even something as seemingly innocuous as lingerie catalogs can serve as an open-door enticement to young boys, drawing them into a pursuit of increasingly graphic stimulation. Do you really want to open that door?

I didn't start out to write a chapter of dos and don'ts. And I'm sure some of you don't want to hear this. But if you really want to know what factors I see interfering with sexual relationships, pornography is at (or near) the top of the list. If a guy is getting visually stimulated by sexual material, it will affect his relationship with his wife.

Before you think I'm being too tough on you guys, I need to give women equal grief. It's just as demeaning, though perhaps more subtly damaging, when a wife says,

"I can't wait to see Tom Selleck on TV tonight." Or when a group of women ooh and ahh about the way Brad Pitt or some other young celebrity looked without his shirt on in his last movie. This is a backhanded slap at the men they are with. Guys are expected to laugh off such talk. But I don't think you can do that—at least not completely. A little piece of thorn is always left in there to fester.

My own personal experience is not the only thing that has convinced me of pornography's threat to the marriage relationship. A friend called some months ago to ask me to pray for her husband, who had become so addicted to pornography that it was destroying their relationship. This is a frequent confession heard at Promise Keepers conferences; countless men are struggling in this area.

One of the most articulate discussions of this came from a man who shared his story in the book, *Power of a Promise Kept.* When he finally recognized and admitted his addiction to pornography, he says he also gained a painful understanding of how his behavior had affected his wife, Martha, and their relationship: "I realized God gave me a certain amount of sexual and relational energy. And he gave Martha her own commensurate needs. There should have been a direct correlation between the two. But because I was wasting a certain amount of my sexual interest and energy on the side for so many years, Martha had experienced a real deficiency in the attention and focused energy she'd received from me. I began to realize I needed to accept responsibility for that failure, and I determined to turn that around.

"For too long, instead of understanding my wife's sexual needs and working to meet them, I'd convinced myself that my own tolerance for sexual frustration was lower than hers, that my own needs were greater. If we hadn't made love for a week or so, I'd think, *Well, for crying out loud, I obviously need more sex than she does.* That would become rationalization for masturbation or for stimulation from pornography.

"Whenever Martha wanted to be intimate and I was already spent, it was a smack in the face because it made what I was giving up so obvious. The real thing with her was always better than any counterfeit or fantasy. The only true appeal of the fantasy was that it was always available—and without the work a real relationship took. It was simpler and easier. But it was always second best."

We live in a visual age where we're not merely exposed to unprecedented sexual imagery, we're practically overwhelmed with it. Is it merely a coincidence that so many marriages are in trouble today? Pornography is an insidious plan of the enemy to frustrate the marriage bed and destroy relationships by tarnishing something meant to be precious and replacing it with a cheap imitation that is "always second best." So if you allow sexually explicit or sexually provocative material in your house, or entertain it in your mind, you are opening a door to a danger that could have serious, long-lasting impact on you, your sexual relationship, and maybe even your children.

SELF-IMAGE

One of the main things that makes sex a touchy subject for me is my constant battle with weight and the corresponding struggle I have with self-esteem. This struggle started for me during my very first pregnancy. At about five months I began to get hungry for the first time in my life. No one had prepared me for the feelings I'd have or the changes that would take place in my body—inside or out.

I couldn't understand how it happened, but I managed to give birth to Timothy without losing a pound of the weight I'd gained during pregnancy. I was so distressed that in the weeks and months that followed, I would lie in bed at night next to Randy, wishing more than anything else in the world that I could somehow crawl out of the body I was now in and be the same person I used to be. When I looked in a mirror, I couldn't stand what I saw. This strange new "family-size" shell didn't represent me. I felt real shame and hatred for my own body.

And I've never been happy with my body since. I continue to struggle with my weight and even more with the negative feelings I have because of it.

I know that men are stimulated by what they see. My husband is a man. So on some level, sometimes it may only be subconscious, I worry that he can't possibly, really, truly find me attractive anymore. Not in *this* body.

I'm not the only woman in the world who feels this way. And I'm not the first to come up short (and wide) when I measure my own appearance against the lean, leggy look of all those models who show up on TV, in magazine ads, and on billboards everywhere.

So if you're wondering why she sometimes fails to respond sexually the way she used to, why it's been so long since she wore lacy nightgowns, why she now prefers the lights off when you make love and often pulls away at your unexpected touch, she may have a real hatred and distaste for her own body.

What can you do to help? Well, that's a tough one.

In weak moments of questionable sanity, I have asked my dear husband to help me by encouraging me to exercise. But when he sets about doing just that, no matter how tactfully or gently he approaches the issue, I find myself thinking, *He must be so totally disgusted and turned off by my body that he wants me to work out!* So the poor guy can't win for losing.

Ultimately I know that this is *my* problem and that I'm my own worst enemy. It all boils down to how I feel about myself at the very core of my being.

So what helps more than anything else is when I'm feeling affirmed in other areas of my life. When Randy whispers sweet nothings about something other than my appearance—how much he appreciates such and such about me, how much I blessed him by doing this or that—this warms my heart and makes me want to be tender toward him.

What I am saying is this: Here is a critical opportunity for you to apply Paul's principle of "preferring one another" by putting your wife's feelings ahead of your own, by considering her perspective and not just yours.

A big part of the problem here, for men and for women, is that we have unrealistic expectations. We've all bought into the modern media's measure of physical attractiveness. Few women, and even fewer men, are prepared for the natural changes that occur with time and physical maturity.

So it often comes as a shock to the wife as well as her husband to learn that childbirth changes her physiology forever. She can't help it. That's the way God made her. Is she going to have to feel bad about her looks and herself for the rest of her life because of it?

She just might unless she can feel affirmed and loved unconditionally by a husband who prefers her and considers her needs more important than his own.

I'm not suggesting you men be insincere any more than I'm suggesting you should ignore the fact if your wife has a serious weight problem. But I am saying this is an even touchier issue for most of us women than most of you men understand. So the approach you take will make all the difference.

You'll need to be extremely sensitive and gentle in the approach you take. Even if your true motivation is concern for your wife's health and need for exercise, you're a lot better off casually asking, "Honey, how would you like to take a walk together after supper?" than suggesting "Why don't we start a four-day-a-week walking program?" Better she suppose "He wants to spend some time together talking" than "He thinks I'm so overweight he wants to change me."

I'm not proposing deceit or manipulation here. I think it's more a matter of sensitivity and consideration—which is required in great measure in this issue.

RUNNING ON EMPTY

There's another almost mundane reason that sex is such a touchy subject. I decided to include it here after a recent discussion I had in the back of a New York City taxi. I'd caught the cab with two married, professional women, who also happened to be mothers. We were discussing this book, so I gave them a quick summary of the basic outline. When I came to this chapter, I listed all the answers I've given thus far why sex can be such a touchy subject. One of the women spoke up to say: "What about 'just being too tired'?" And the three of us immediately agreed that the fatigue factor had often been an issue for all of us.

If your spouse no longer responds the way you wish she would, the explanation may be simple: She may be exhausted.

If that's the case, your first step in solving the problem should be just as simple: Tune in and help shoulder some of the load. Redistribute some of the weight of responsibility in your family. Invest a little more of your energy around the house and with the kids; in return, you may be the recipient of a little more of her energy and affection in bed at night.

But redistributing responsibility may not be enough to relieve the exhaustion. You may also need to reorder your priorities.

When you first got married, if anyone had suggested you and your spouse should pull out your appointment calendars or your personal planners each week to schedule times for personal intimacy, you would have laughed. But many couples out there could revitalize their sex lives if they would try this.

Most of us need to make intimacy a higher priority. That takes time as well as energy. And sometimes both of those things require a little planning.

Kids have a big impact on priorities and on the fatigue factor as well. When children enter into the equation, all too often romance and intimacy get shouldered aside. We focus so much love and affection and concern on the kids that the marriage is left to stagnate—or worse. The kids have needs. And because they are kids, most of these needs can't wait. Our spouse on the other hand, as an adult, *can* wait. So we make him. And if we're not careful, our relationship becomes a lesser priority.

Of course sometimes a child's needs have to take priority. I'm not advocating child neglect or selfishness here. Just a note of caution.

It took Randy and me a long time to figure this out. We needed someone to provide us a reality check. We needed to remember before our kids were, *we* were. *We* were in the circle before anyone else was. *We* should never have allowed anyone to come between the two of us.

For those who get married after a child is already in the equation, it's not too late to start a new tradition, to make certain you keep each other first priority, and to allow the child to take second place. This doesn't mean your parental love is any less—just that your priorities are in proper sync.

Too many couples invest all their best time, energy, and resources in their children. And when the kids are gone, they don't have a clue who the person is sleeping next to them. Unfortunately, for more than may want to admit it, the children have been a welcome excuse, an escape from having to be truly intimate with a mate.

TRANSLATING THE "I" WORD

The final possible reason I'm going to suggest for sex being such a touchy issue is a common one: many of us have a lousy understanding of intimacy.

We too often confuse sex with intimacy in much the same way we confuse lust and love. This happens when we think of intimacy only in physical terms—and fail to understand that it really involves so much more. It's an easy mistake to make in our day and age because our culture regularly portrays and celebrates the physical side of intimacy while ignoring (and even denying) the emotional and spiritual dimensions. That only serves to compound the problem for many men who are uncomfortable dealing with or expressing emotions anyway. Reinforce and validate their natural tendencies with society's attitudes, and it's not surprising that so many women say they are frustrated by a lack of intimacy in their marriages.

For women intimacy is not only physical. It's also (sometimes mostly) emotional. Sex can be great. But it's only part of intimacy which for most women includes and requires respect, trust, and open communication of thoughts and feelings. To a woman, intimacy is a connection of hearts more than a connection of bodies.

Men who understand this often make another wonderful discovery. Women who have their needs for intimacy met, are much more sexually responsive.

Another secret some guys never learn: a large measure of intimacy can be expressed through physical affection given generously with no sexual strings attached. Behavioral scientists tell us all human beings need to be touched. They still can't explain what can no longer be denied: There is real power in human touch. Whether public or private, seemingly small displays of loving affection—holding hands, an arm draped around a shoulder, snuggling close on a car seat, a park bench, or a couch—can help create and foster a powerful sense of intimacy. Women who receive affection at other times will probably be more sexually responsive at bedtime.

I think it's incredibly ironic that Christians are often branded as prudish and anti-sex; we're considered too restrictive and uptight to approve of, let alone enjoy, sex. The truth is, we're uniquely positioned to know and appreciate sexual intimacy in the fullest sense.

This is what a friend of mine was getting at one day when he said, "Before we can be intimate, we have to know how to express intimacy."

That sounds profound. What did he mean? Or maybe the better question is, *How do we do that?* How do we express loving intimacy?

Here again Christians have the advantage because we have the perfect model of love and intimacy from the author/creator of love and intimacy. This was the selfless, sacrificing model the apostle Paul spelled out for Christians, particularly for husbands and wives, in that fifth chapter of his letter to the Ephesians. Consider this excerpt from Eugene Peterson's *The Message,* which puts that passage in contemporary language:

> Out of respect for Christ, be courteously reverent to one another.
>   Wives, understand and support your husbands in ways that show your support to Christ. The husband provides leadership to his wife the way Christ does to his church, not by domineering but by cherishing. So just as the church submits to Christ as he exercises such leadership, wives should likewise submit to their husbands.

Husbands, go all out in love for your wives, exactly as Christ did for the church—a love marked by giving, not getting. Christ's love makes the church whole. His words evoke her beauty. Everything he does and says is designed to bring the best out of her, dressing her in dazzling white silk, radiant with holiness. And that is how husbands ought to love their wives. They are really doing themselves a favor—since they're already "one" in marriage.

No one abuses his own body, does he? No, he feeds and pampers it. That's how Christ treats us, the church, since we are part of his body.... This is a huge mystery, and I don't pretend to understand it all. What is clearest to me is the way Christ treats the church. And this provides a good picture of how each husband is to treat his wife, loving himself in loving her, and how each wife is to honor her husband.

The more I read and contemplate this passage, the more I understand my relationship to God and the more I appreciate my relationship with my husband—the clearer I see the parallels between the two relationships. And the more inspired this imagery seems.

To help us feebleminded, finite creatures grasp the infinite truth of Christ's sacrificial love and commitment for the church, God used the simple, human, everyday example of a bride and bridegroom, a wife and a husband. He made a theologically complex and sacred concept more simple.

But I think we also need to look at this imagery from the opposite angle. In comparing a marriage relationship to Christ's perfect sacrificial love, God is raising the relational standard for us by making something so simple and commonplace (marriage) into something mysteriously sacred and special.

What better laboratory than the marriage bed for us to learn the critical spiritual skill of "preferring one another" in love? How much easier it is to be intimate with a spouse if we first know what it means to be emotionally and spiritually intimate (honest, open, vulnerable, giving) with a heavenly Father. Only after we understand and embrace and accept God's intimate love for us can we begin to have that same attitude in our human relationships.

What we're talking about here is a no-strings-attached kind of love. An attitude that says "I didn't expect, I don't expect, and I won't expect anything from you. I just love you and want you to know that." That kind of love naturally creates a desire for intimacy. I know because that's what happened to Randy and me.

As my own painful history was brought out into the open in counseling, and as Randy began to understand the effect those experiences had on me and my perceptions of sex, he became more compassionate, more patient with me. The last thing Randy wanted to do was to add to the problem by being seen as another perpetrator, another selfish person who just wanted something from me. He became an even greater servant leader than he'd been to me before. He waited for me, and he loved me unconditionally, without demand or expectation. Finally I began to respond to his love instead of reacting to my old history. And I finally reached the point I could write this song:

A Child of the Secret
She's got herself a history that carries secret shame
On the outside she can wear a smile, but sorrow's
*　her middle name*
She's borne her pain for many years, since she was
*　but a child*
No one knew, or had a clue
This girl had been defiled.

Oh, she sold herself in search of love
And gave up who she was

To try and please those around her
All for the need of love.

She's felt real dirty and unclean—
Hated who she is.
She can't let people get too close—
even lost the will to live.

Oh, she sold herself in search of love
And gave up who she was
To try and please those around her
All for the need of love.
To try and please those around her
All for the need of love.

Well, salvation has come her way
For He has known her shame.
His desire is to set her free, and wash away her pain.

No more does she sell herself,
Or give up who she is.
For Love has finally found her out,
And now she is His.
For Love has finally found her out,
And now she is His.

Oh she was a child of the secret, but now she is His.
Oh she was a child of the secret, but now ...
She is His.

I remember lying in bed next to my husband on our honeymoon. As I watched him sleeping and listened to his peaceful breathing, I very clearly sensed God saying to me, *I'm going to use Randy to show you my love for you!* At that point in my life I could never have imagined how long the lesson would take to sink in, or what a slow learner I'd turn out to be.

It's only been since I wrote that song in 1991 that I've been able to fully accept God's love for me or to fully enjoy the intimacy of my husband's love. But it's been worth the wait. I am very aware that the wait has been difficult for Randy to endure at times, but I have hope the second half of our marriage will more than make up for everything.

Today when someone asks me, "Why does sex always have to be such a touchy subject?" I can finally say, "It doesn't have to be."

SO WHAT DOES SHE WANT FROM YOU, ANYWAY?

She wants you to:

- Put her needs first in your sexual relationship.
- Dedicate yourself to sexual purity—exclusively for her.
- Be willing to work at making your sexual relationship the very best it can be—no more shortcuts.
- Consistently demonstrate your love for her and your desire to express that love in every way possible—including sex.
- Be sensitive in understanding that there may be deeper issues—and provide opportunities to talk about them.

part **2**

What Can I Do to Win Her Back?

chapter **7**

Is There Any Hope?
It All Must Begin
with a Change in Heart

We've spent most of a book thus far trying to answer common questions I've heard asked by men who want to understand what has gone wrong in their relationships with women. But understanding the problem, as important as that is, just isn't enough. Recognizing the mistakes of the past, even admitting there *were* mistakes made in the past, may not be enough.

Most of the men who have come to me for counsel or encouragement know that. So they are also asking the $64,000 questions: "Now what?" "How do I win her back?" and "What can I do to make things better?"

One man wrote to say: "I am one of life's failures. I ran away from my church, my wife, and my children. As a result, I am despised by my family. My church has allowed me back; God is forgiving. But women and children often are not. Please help me ... How can I regain their trust?"

Another man wrote to say he'd made some major changes in his life, but "my marriage is still in trouble. My wife has rejected every effort I have made to be a promise keeper to her. She has seen a change in me and loves the father I have become to our children. But she still says she just doesn't want me to be a part of her life right now."

Analysis and explanation have a place, to be sure. But these writers, like most men I talk to, are itching for action. They're fixers. They want practical steps they can take. Clear examples they can follow. Simple suggestions they can put into practice. They need handles of hope they can hang onto. In other words, they want to know what they can *do*.

So that's just what we're going to provide in this section.

Most of you have been eager to reach this point since you first opened the book. Some of you probably skipped or scanned your way through part one to get here.

I understand your feelings. From the first day I started writing, I've wanted nothing more than to skip out of the first section of this book to where we are now. I too have a tough time focusing on past problems—when Randy and I missed the mark, where other couples' struggles and scenarios looked bleak. I didn't decide to write this book because I wanted to remember the mistakes of the past or to obsess about what is wrong with relationships. But recognition and understanding had to come first. Only then could I offer encouragement, practical help, and hope to all of you who long for another chance to do better.

I want you to know hope, to see the light at the end of the tunnel. I realize that none of us has all the answers for everyone else. Life is a growth process, and I hope we don't stop learning and growing until we die.

In Randy's and my case, I can honestly say that in the years of our youth we made many mistakes. We didn't have the benefit of strong role models. We attended and only too recently graduated from the school of hard knocks, and we don't enjoy thinking back to those "good ol' days" that aren't so old and weren't so good. But if others can learn from our shortcomings and our failures, then I'll count the painful review well worthwhile.

Some of the practical lessons we've learned in recent years can easily be applied by others. That's why I'm much more excited about sharing a number of more positive and hopeful stories. And that's what I intend to do as we attempt to answer a few more questions men are asking. Questions like ...

Is there any hope? How do I get her to respect me? What can I do to show her I really care? What does she *need* from me, anyway?

So don't quit now. Things are so much better for the Phillips today. And we believe they can be better for you.

IS THERE ANY HOPE?

There was a time when, if you had asked this question about my marriage, honesty would have compelled me to admit, "No. I don't feel like there is." On my most upbeat days I could have only managed a discouraged, "I just don't know."

So when broken, hurting, discouraged guys approach me at Promise Keepers conferences to tell me their stories and ask, "Is there any hope?" I know how they are feeling. Randy and I have been there.

But no more!

Today when a discouraged man asks, "Is there any hope?" I don't hesitate for one second. "Yes! There's hope!" I say with confidence. Because, in these past few years, I myself have found hope. I don't downplay the seriousness of their problems. I try never to mislead them into thinking the solutions will be simple or painless. I certainly won't promise them an easy road out of their predicament. But when anyone asks, "Is there any hope?" I definitely can offer them some.

PROMISE KEEPERS

Let me tell you what happened on two different levels simultaneously.

First, much of the hope I have today stems directly from what I've been privileged to observe through my involvement with the Promise Keepers movement itself.

I will never forget my experience as a volunteer at the very first PK conference back in 1991 at the Events Center on the University of Colorado campus. I was overwhelmed by the sight of 4,200 men who had come to that place with the single, sincere desire to worship God together— unashamedly. I'd never seen anything like it in all my life. These guys joined hands and sang with strength and passion. Then they broke into small groups to open up their hearts to each other.

As I watched those men during that conference, I felt an undeniable awareness of God's presence in this profound event. In their attitudes and actions I could see power and a potential that gave me, as a woman, a very real sense of security and protection, and an even greater feeling of encouragement and hopefulness.

This first PK conference took place at about the same time Robert Bly's book *Iron John* was making headlines and prompting widespread media speculation on how a burgeoning men's movement might change the face of our society. But that interest soon died down, perhaps as it became evident to men that *significant* transformation (for individuals or society) would require more than an occasional retreat in the woods to beat drums, bond with "the boys," and thereby rediscover the "true" meaning of masculinity.

Meanwhile, the Promise Keepers movement continued to grow. The next year 22,000 men gathered in Boulder, and then in the summer of 1993 52,000 men from all over the country converged on Boulder's Folsom Field for a weekend conference. As the years progressed I found even more reason for hope. In 1994, more than 270,000 men attended six conferences in cities around the United States; in 1995, thirteen conferences drew more than 725,000 men; and in 1996 over twenty conferences drew over a million men. As we go to press with this book, another twenty-plus conferences are scheduled for 1997. And preparations are going on for an assembly on the national mall in Washington, D.C., on October 4, 1997. A multitude of men will converge to pray and ask God's forgiveness for the injustices, racism, and rebellion we have engaged in since our nation began.

So the fire continues to spread. And as it has, I've observed five key things happening in the Promise Keepers movement throughout these years—five distinctives that have given me greater and greater reason for hope in my own marriage *and* in the relationships of those men who come to me concerned and worried, asking, "Is it too late?"

1. Mentoring

Men are receiving godly teaching and guidance. At the conferences, speakers of substance, integrity, and years of proven character are delivering messages of instruction, encouragement, and hope. Often their words are pointed, but they are always without condemnation. And before they go home from those conferences men are encouraged to find other men they can share with and learn from, examples they can follow when they need further wisdom and guidance.

2. Brokenness

Men are confessing sins they had given themselves over to for years. Some are being overwhelmed with sorrow for their neglect and abandonment of their wives and families. Others are being deeply convicted for having abdicated their leadership and placed undue responsibilities and pressures on spouses whose shoulders could not bear them alone.

3. Camaraderie

Men sense they are no longer isolated and alone. They are strengthened by the presence of thousands of men from all over the nation. They've become aware that they aren't the only men on the face of the earth struggling with tough issues such as fear and failure.

4. Vision

Men are leaving stadiums energized with a renewed vision and determination to grow spiritually and to improve all their relationships—with God, with their wives and families, and with their friends. For many men, it is the first time in their lives they've had *any* kind of vision or sense of purpose.

5. Reconciliation

Last, but definitely not least, men are beginning to embrace the biblical mandate of reconciliation. God has been doing a miracle in tearing down walls that divide us in the church—racially *and* denominationally. It has been obvious to all of us who have labored at Promise Keepers that the Lord is determined to bring his church to a place of unity. And I'm convinced that includes a new unity between men and women—between husbands and wives. Because I've seen it happen—in my own marriage and in countless others.

Having said all this about Promise Keepers, I need to make something very clear. I wouldn't presume, and don't intend, to say that Promise Keepers is *the* only hope for every troubled relationship out there. Neither do I want to imply it's the only place where you'll find these five ingredients that seem so key to the movement and to the hope Randy and I have found. But these five keys play a critical role in the changes taking place in the hearts and lives and relationships of men across the country—including the man of my life.

These observations and conclusions are what I tried to communicate to men when asked to speak to the 1995 conferences; I wanted to give them a fresh understanding of what they are experiencing by offering a view from one woman's perspective. But my number-one goal has always been to encourage men who are disheartened and perhaps tempted to give up because they are short on hope.

A SPEECH FULL OF HOPE

Every time I addressed a stadium full of men I told them this:

> Many of you who are married will find that your wives are overjoyed about your experiences at the conference. They are eager to support you in your enthusiasm and your renewed vision.
>
> Others of you will find your wives cautious, hesitant, and uneasy. Perhaps they will be a little undone by the strange, changed man who walks through the door when you get home. Your kids may respond likewise. Please don't be surprised or caught off guard by this reaction. It's normal.
>
> The problem may have to do with change. We women have a difficult time with it—even when we've prayed for it for years. It presses our comfort zone. Sometimes we're more willing to cling to what is familiar—even if it is miserable—rather than have our lives

turned upside down and inside out. At least with the familiar we know what to expect.

Some of you will return home to have your enthusiasm and zeal met with blank stares. You must understand the hearts of these wives. Likely they have been waiting and hoping for a long time, praying so hard, daring to hope one time too many. And now their hearts have grown cold and indifferent, and they have told themselves that it's too late. They don't have any strength or hope left. Their trust levels have been severely compromised.

Please do not lose heart. Stay the course. Get in a small group and become accountable. You may find support there.

At the same time, while a small group can provide you encouragement, please be careful not to allow it to take the place of your wife. You may need to prepare yourself for a few *years* of commitment, patience, and prayer before your wife and family realize that you are "for real."

But if the merchant in Jesus' parable was willing to buy the whole field for one pearl of great price, he must have thought the pearl worth the price required (Matthew 13:45–46). Could it be that your wife is a "pearl" who is worth the cost required of you?

Perhaps this analogy will help. A prizefighter enters the ring with his contender. His contender wants to strip him of the title. When the prizefighter strikes and connects with his punches, his contender isn't going to simply stand there and take it. He's going to fight back. You are that prizefighter. Satan is your contender. He wants to strip you of all your titles—husband, father, man of integrity.

But remember, there are those in your corner who will wipe away the sweat from your brow, blot the blood from your wounds, give you fresh water, and speak words of encouragement to you. These encouragers are Jesus (your number-one fan and trainer), your small group, your closest friends, and yes, your wife, as she catches the vision and sees the worth and value of you—her prizefighter.

Please hear this, as I have never said anything with more sincerity. On behalf of the women that you men represent—sisters, moms, daughters, and wives.

I ask your forgiveness for not showing you the respect you deserve.

I ask your forgiveness for the demeaning and belittling words that we have uttered.

I apologize for the ways we've coddled and smothered you with our protectiveness, thereby emasculating you. We've done it in ignorance. (Understand that mothering comes naturally to us; it is our God-designed makeup. We have simply misappropriated our calling when we've tried to mother you.)

We are proud of you for standing for the Lord and desiring to make a difference. Thank you for making the effort to become the best leaders, best husbands, best fathers, and best of friends. We love you.

A REAL TRANSFORMATION

I'm able to offer those words of encouragement and hope only because I've found hope myself. And as I said earlier, that discovery has taken place on two levels simultaneously. You see, over the past few years, during the same time I've been so encouraged by the growth and impact of Promise Keepers, I've discovered even more reason for hope in my own personal life—through the growth and changes that have taken place in Randy, in me, and in our marriage.

Finally, here's the hopeful part of our story which actually began at the most hopeless point in our marriage.

The change really began with Randy during a three-day period in July 1990. I didn't know what was going on at the time. At first I thought Randy was physically sick. He couldn't eat for three days. He couldn't sleep. He looked awful. I worried that he was seriously ill.

When I realized he was just as sick in spirit, I did not know what to think. Was he depressed? Here was my husband, looking absolutely beaten, totally withdrawing from me and our children, spending his entire holiday weekend sitting silently by himself, or lying motionless in bed.

It scared me.

I kept asking, "Are you okay?" At first, all he would say was "I don't know. I don't know." And that scared me, too.

Finally he said, "God is doing something very deep in my life right now. And I just can't talk about it yet."

This is a spiritual crisis? That realization may have eased my fears a little. But I don't think it improved my understanding one bit. I still couldn't imagine what was going on inside my husband. I may never completely understand, as this was a very personal and defining moment in his life.

Randy's Story

It helps to hear Randy's perspective as he looks back and remembers those days of crisis in these words:

> We'd just gotten home from our family's summer vacation. As I did every year, I'd planned what I thought would be a great cross-country vacation— always bigger and better than the one the year before. This one had turned out to be so terrible that I felt like I'd wasted two and a half weeks of our lives. Holly and I weren't getting along. The kids felt and heard the conflict. Mechanical troubles, bad weather, scheduling problems, and a money shortage left me wondering if we'd become the basis for the next "vacation" movie starring Chevy Chase. Whenever I refer back to this as the "vacation from hell," I get a hearty "amen" from the family.

When we got home, the impossible happened. Life got even worse. Tension escalated on the home front. Problems plagued the ministry I was overseeing. My entire life seemed about to come crashing down around me. I cried out to God in my helplessness, and he did not answer. It was like praying into a void.

For three horrible days it was as if he totally abandoned me—leaving me completely to myself. I didn't understand because I'd never experienced anything like it. Only looking back can I conclude that he let me feel that way to show me what my life would be like without him. How, if I was left to my own devices, my own strength, my life would be an even bigger disaster than the vacation I had so tediously planned.

I quickly realized three important things:

1. How empty life would be apart from Jesus.

2. How important Holly and my family were to me—how much I loved and needed them.

3. How my life was devoid of real friendships. I realized if I would die of a heart attack the next day, the six guys who carried my casket out of the church would have to be men who had never helped carry me when I was alive. Holly and I had no real intimate friendships, no heart-to-heart involvement with other people who loved and cared about us.

By the end of those three days of wandering through my own personal wilderness, I realized that God had been there all along—silently waiting and allowing me to recognize and feel some very deep, disturbing truths about my own life.

I determined before that holiday ended that I needed to make some major changes in my life.

A Time to Forgive

Randy went through this wilderness experience at the same time Bill McCartney became convinced of the need for Promise Keepers. Within one year Randy left the pastorate and accepted the invitation to become president of this fledgling organization. I attribute a lot of the gradual change that took place within Randy to that move.

Looking back, I can see also that Randy was going through a real transformation with the Lord. He realized he could no longer go on living the second half of his life the way he had lived the first half. He realized he didn't have friends because he held people at bay. And slowly he began to really *see* me. Randy was thinking about the future in a new way. He had decided relationships and life needed to go deeper than they ever had before. He'd started viewing me, the kids, everything—differently. But at that time I was too swallowed up by my own discouragement to really notice what was happening with my husband. I was just starting counseling and still hadn't begun to deal with the issues that would culminate a few months later on that evening I call "the night of the stoplights."

After that night, when I finally unloaded a lifetime of hurt, the following days are nothing more than a foggy, emotional blur in my memory. I went through the motions of daily routines with Randy and the kids. But I was an empty shell. I had no emotions—nothing—left inside.

We both felt so discouraged that when our fifteenth anniversary arrived a few days later, neither of us had made or suggested any plans to celebrate it. Despite the fact that we'd always made a big deal of anniversaries, I didn't even get Randy a gift. I didn't have it in me to even make the effort. I didn't care anymore.

Evidently Randy didn't either, because the entire day went by without him making any reference to our anniversary. Evening finally came. After we'd put the kids to bed, Randy approached me and asked if I would join him in our bedroom.

I figured he wanted the inevitable, and thought, *No way that's going to happen!*

So when he asked me to lie down on the bed with him, all my defenses were up. That's when he caught me by surprise, saying, "Holly, I want to give you your anniversary present now. But before I do, I don't want you to feel like you have to respond."

I thought, *What is going on here?* I knew Randy could tell I wasn't angry, I was emotionless. To me everything had been said. It seemed there was nothing left—of us.

"Holly," Randy said, "would you please forgive me for all the years and all the thoughtless things that I did, for all the immaturity I exhibited, for all of the times I didn't support you, those times I didn't love you the way you needed to be loved. Can you ever find it in your heart to forgive me?"

At that point we were lying on our bed, sideways, almost nose to nose. I heard what he said. I looked into his face as he watched my reaction. For a long time, I couldn't say anything. At last I replied, "Randy, I just can't give you a response right now."

"That's okay," he assured me, "you don't need to. But I want you to know that I now see a lot of what I've done, and I want you to forgive me. All those times I made you worry about our finances. When you worried that our electricity would be turned off. All the different things that I've done ..."

And he went down a list that included most of the incidents I'd recalled on the infamous "night of the stoplights."

I sensed Randy's sorrow was genuine. But I didn't know if our marriage could recover. Was it too late? I couldn't muster up the feeling myself anymore. I had nothing left. If it wasn't too late, if our relationship was ever going to be healed, it was only going to be through the grace of God. He was going to have to be the doctor who put this thing back together again. The Lord was going to have to apply divine defibrillator paddles to jump-start my heart. I couldn't save myself or revive our marriage.

I could only say, "I'm sorry, Randy, but I don't know if or when I can forgive you." I said it calmly. Without bitterness. Without any real feeling at all.

After thinking a while longer, I finally added, "I can try. I don't know what it's going to take. But I do know this, Randy. We'll never be the same."

"That's okay," he whispered. "That's okay. We don't want to be."

A little later he asked if he could hug me, and I said, "Yeah."

I was nothing more than a rag doll in his arms that evening.

Everything wasn't better the next morning. No sudden miracle transformed our marriage. I still didn't have any real hope. In fact, I didn't *feel* any different.

But in the days and weeks that followed I did sense a difference in Randy. In fact, I finally began to recognize some of the change that had been taking place in his heart ever since that Fourth of July weekend the previous summer.

One of the first changes I noticed was a subtle but significant shift in our communication patterns. For most of our marriage, when there was something wrong in our relationship, it seemed I was the only one who noticed. I was always the one to bring problems up for discussion, usually with intense anger. In his frustration, Randy would retreat—emotionally and even physically by going to bed, pulling up the covers, and falling asleep—hoping the whole thing would blow over and be done with when he woke up the next morning. In my frustration, I'd storm downstairs, lie on the couch, and lose sleep. I felt I was the only one who wanted to see our problems get resolved. It seemed Randy never thought they were so serious he couldn't sleep them off.

That pattern had changed, though, as I'd gradually lost confidence in Randy, myself, and our relationship. Now I was the one withdrawing emotionally—going to bed and pulling the covers over my head—not wanting to make the effort to communicate, because it seemed hopeless.

But in the weeks following Randy's anniversary apology, I noticed a shift in that pattern. Now *he* was the one pursuing the issue, initiating communication. And he was always so gentle in the way he did it. He'd say, "Honey, let's sit down and talk. It's going to be okay." I was afraid of confrontation and pain, but he would assure me, "It's okay. I'm not going to get upset with you. Just tell me what's *really* going on."

When I began to gradually open up, I realized my own communication was now different. I was no longer railing and accusing in my tone. I was no longer angry, bitter, and berating. I no longer tried to wield words as weapons. No fire, no heat, no hate was left to do that. I no longer wanted to hurt Randy with what I said, but I didn't try to protect him either—at my own expense. I simply stated the truth.

And he listened. That may have been the biggest change. He really listened. He was no longer defensive. God had changed his heart so he could finally hear and receive what I had to say.

As Randy recounts it:

> For months God had been showing me that Holly was close to hardening her heart against me. That scared me. But even more than that, it made me sad. So by the time she came home from counseling that night and unloaded the emotional baggage she'd been carrying, I knew I couldn't argue. I realized what she was saying was right. I didn't hear Holly *accusing* me anymore, but rather I felt a deep sense of God revealing the truth through her. When I looked at the person I loved most in life, I recognized the pain and suffering she was going through—and I realized how much I'd contributed to that. How much of her hurt could be

directly traced to my lack of honor and love for her. And it broke my heart.

I began to see Holly in a new light—as God saw her. I realized what she could have been like if I'd given her the love and protection and affirmation she needed. That knowledge pierced me and made me even more determined to change—really change.

I sensed, more than I really understood, the change in Randy's heart. It wasn't as if he'd become a martyr saying, "Okay, whip me with the truth!" But he did take the ultimate risk by laying himself bare. He let me know he was willing to have me say whatever he *needed* to hear.

We had a lot of talks in the days and weeks and months that followed. Many things surfaced that we'd both buried over the years. But Randy was quick to acknowledge any newly revealed wrongs. And he'd ask my forgiveness as soon as they came to light.

I soon discovered that when someone assumes a spirit of humility and willingly acknowledges what they've done, it takes the hot, angry wind out of your sails. When you can sense their genuine sorrow—it's like shutting down the burner that heats a hot-air balloon. Immediately the balloon begins to sink slowly back to earth.

Every time we'd have a healthy conversation, and Randy would see something or ask my forgiveness for another incident one of us remembered, it was like a warm breeze blowing across my heart of ice. I gradually began to melt. God was performing a heart transplant, one memory at a time. He ever so slowly transformed my heart of anger into a heart of compassion for my husband. Each time something surfaced, the Lord would help me see that Randy never received the training to know how to deal with that situation—he'd had no significant role models in his adult life. He wasn't intentional in his insensitivity, oversight, or neglect. As I learned to view Randy through

God's eyes, I began to see past *my* pain to his. And I found an ever-growing measure of forgiveness that eventually blossomed into a new, rich, beautiful love. In turn, Randy also experienced new freedom to speak truth to me in love.

NO QUICK FIX

So … *is there any hope?*

When men ask me that question today I tell them, "There's always hope! With God it's never too late."

I honestly believe that. And I think that's where all hope starts.

With God.

Any real hope for our relationships (or our lives) has a spiritual basis. But all too often that's the last direction we look.

A good friend of mine likes to remind me that most of us have the attitude, *When all else fails, pray.* The truth is, we ought to *Pray, so nothing else fails.* It's in the spiritual realm that we find true help and hope.

This was certainly true for Randy and me. Nothing could change in our relationship until a change took place in our hearts. Spiritual healing had to precede the healing of our relationship.

I know many guys are discouraged and have lost hope wondering, "How long am I going to have to pay for my mistakes?" While I don't want to discourage them further, I know I have to be honest. So I warn them, "It's going to take time. A couple of years maybe."

Before they get too depressed about that, I tell them, "Don't give up. Get plugged into a small group of guys who can encourage and help you move from good intentions to loving actions. And give God permission to work through your life. Change those areas that you realize need addressing—let him have his way with you. Let it be in his timing, and your life will shine. Hopefully, she'll see the change and slowly be won over."

Honesty also compels me to say, "There are no guarantees, because we all have wills. She may choose not to respond. You can't control that. You may have to let go of her—open your arms and trust God. He's a big God. If you're holding on too hard and squeezing the life out of your spouse, you may have to let go and give God time and room to work."

Most guys are sobered by what I tell them. But a lot of them will still want to know, "What changes can I make? I'll try anything! Tell me, what can I DO?"

To them and to you I say this: Many changes may need to be made. I'll even suggest some specific changes Randy and others have made in the remaining chapters of this section. Changes of attitude. Changes in behavior. Even changes in perspective. But if there's to be any hope, first there must be a change of heart.

You can't go home today and walk in the door with the attitude that you (and/or God) need to change your spouse. *If* you hope for change, start by taking a long, hard, honest look at yourself. Examine what *you* are doing and what *you* have done. Own up to the mistakes you recognize.

And before you walk in that door, pray a prayer like this:

"Lord, I'm giving you my life. I'm going to rely on you to change me. I obviously can't do it in my own strength or resolve, or I'd have done it by now. So remind me of the truth I've heard and learned. I'm giving you my consent to perform surgery on my heart and my life. Do whatever you need to do. I'm not telling you how much anesthesia or what instruments to use. I'm not going to try to tell you how long the surgery should take. I'm just going to crawl up on your operating table and give you permission to do whatever needs to be done to change my heart."

That's what my husband did. God first filled his heart with sorrow. Then he tuned Randy's heart to mine so that

I could finally respond and fall in love with him all over again. It took time. It's still happening. I'm still learning to adore my husband in new ways, to appreciate every little thing about him, because we are both now deeply in love. Maybe really for the first time.

Is there any hope?

If there was hope for Holly and Randy Phillips, there is hope for anyone.

Our marriage left so much to be desired that it once cost my husband his job—now I'm writing a book that just might help to improve relationships.

I once felt like a worthless accessory to my husband's career—now we're full partners in ministry. I used to lie next to my husband in bed at night feeling so hopeless that I cried out to God: *Why do you even let me live?* Now I lie in bed at night next to my husband and pray that God will allow us both to live to a ripe old age so we can have as long as possible on this earth to enjoy our marriage as it was meant to be enjoyed.

Is there any hope?

Absolutely, unequivocally yes! And it begins with a yielded heart.

SO WHAT DOES SHE WANT FROM YOU, ANYWAY?

She wants you to:

- Never stop being a learner.
- Be open in admitting your mistakes.
- Not to try to go it alone. Let others help you.
- Live with a vision for your life, marriage, and family.
- Grow beyond your boundaries of opinion and prejudice.
- Be patient.
- Never lose heart. Let God change you from the inside out.

chapter **8**

How Do I Get Her to Respect Me?

You May Also Require a Change in Attitude

H ow many men have said, "All I want is a little respect! Is that too much to ask?"

Men want respect. That's no secret. That's reasonable. The Bible even instructs wives to respect their husbands. So it shouldn't be surprising that many men are asking the questions: Why doesn't she respect me. How do I get her to respect me?

However, before trying to answer, I want to make sure we're all on the same page. A certain number of guys confuse "respect" with domination; they believe unquestioned obedience is their due. They say, "All I want is a little respect," but what they are really looking for is control.

That's not what we're talking about here!

To respect someone means "to hold them in high regard, to esteem, to honor, to admire and to value them, and to be willing to defer to them out of reverence, loyalty, or love." Precious few relationships around today can measure up to these criteria.

Are we setting the bar too high? Is this kind of respect a thing of the past? Or could it be that we've set our standards too low?

How do you get the respect we're talking about here?

In answer to that, allow me to paraphrase that old commercial for an investment company: "We get respect the old-fashioned way. We *earn* it."

And how do you earn it? Certainly not by demanding, asking for, or even expecting respect, but by consistently exhibiting integrity—demonstrating honesty, being dependable, and remaining faithful. Those things are like a magnetic north in drawing respect. So is vulnerability—admitting weakness and acknowledging when we've blown it.

Let's consider each of these basic ingredients of integrity.

DEMONSTRATING HONESTY

Begin with honest disclosure:

First, be honest in your prayers with your heavenly Father. (You may as well, he knows everything anyway. So just consider it "truth practice.") Then, second, be honest in your communication with your wife.

Everything I've learned from personal experience and observation convinces me that God honors the environment of truth. It's his enemy that convinces us to hide, retreat, or become silent.

I learned to lie so well and so often growing up that, by the time I became a teen, lying was second nature. In fact, I was such a habitual liar that I often concocted stories when the truth would have served me just as well.

So when I became a Christian and committed my life to Christ, veracity proved to be a major issue for me. I prided myself on my newly acquired Christian candor. Telling the truth was suddenly important to me because it not only symbolized but also convincingly proved the significant change that had taken place in my life.

So I was hit very hard when the Spirit of God showed me how I'd been lying to my husband for years. Every time Randy noticed something was bothering me and asked, "Holly, what's wrong?" and I told him "Nothing"—I'd been lying. Or when he'd apologize for a wrong, I'd quickly respond, "Oh, it's nothing. No big deal. I forgive you." But in fact it did hurt and I hadn't forgiven him.

I wanted to deny it at first. To argue from my heart, *I wasn't really lying, Lord.* In fact, sometimes my motives for saying "Nothing is wrong" seemed downright unselfish—I didn't want to bother Randy with my problems, or I didn't want to say anything I thought might hurt his feelings. More often I'd say, "Nothing's wrong," to avoid triggering an argument or an unpleasant confrontation. (Christians are supposed to be peacemakers, right?) But by the time our marriage reached the crisis stage, I'd been saying, "Nothing's wrong," for years simply because I could no longer muster up the emotional energy to deal with our problems.

It was only in the wake of Randy's fifteenth anniversary apology, his persistent pursuit of the truth in the weeks and months that followed, his initiation of discussion and his gentle insistence, that I could finally tell him what was really wrong and what I was really thinking and feeling. And I finally realized and acknowledged to God, myself, and my husband that I'd been lying for years. When I was willing to see and speak the truth, real healing could begin in me and in our marriage. I saw firsthand how God indeed honors and blesses and uses truth.

I also know that truth, by exposing deep, painful wounds, can seem unbearable. Yet sometimes wounds that have festered for years need to be opened up and the infection treated, before they can ever really heal.

Not long ago at a conference I met a man who is learning this lesson. He told me, "Over fourteen years ago I had a brief affair. I've regretted it every day of my life since. I'd asked God to forgive me, and I believe he did. But for all those years I could never shake the feeling of an ominous cloud hanging over our marriage. So a couple of years ago I confessed the truth to my wife."

"What happened?" I asked. "How did she react?"

"Not well at all." He sadly shook his head at the memory. "I'd hoped the time that had passed would soften the blow. Perhaps it did somewhat. But she still took it hard.

"I wanted her to understand it had only happened once. A single, long-ago indiscretion. An exception to the rule of our relationship.

"But she suddenly wondered if there had ever been anything honest about our entire marriage. Fourteen years' worth of trust was shattered. Gone. It's been almost two years now since I told her, and I'm still rebuilding that trust."

He told me he'd gone to counseling at his wife's request. He'd done everything she'd asked of him. He even joined a small group of Christian men, admitted his transgression to them, and made himself accountable to their guidance and direction. Anything he could think of that might prove himself to her, he was willing to do. He loved his wife that much.

He admitted that the rebuilding process has been harder and longer than he could have imagined. But he insisted, "It's been worth it, Holly. Because the cloud is gone. And my marriage is being rebuilt on a solid foundation of truth."

A short while later I met the man's wife. Knowing he'd talked to me, she confirmed everything he'd said. "It was hard learning the truth," she admits. "And it's been even tougher trusting my husband again. But I'm gradually learning to do that. I'm beginning to realize that if he's been honest about this, I can trust him to be honest about other things as well."

This couple says they are hopeful now that their marriage will recover. After talking with them, I'm confident it will, because God honors truth.

This couple is learning that the price of integrity runs high—perhaps because it's so rare. But it's worth it. Integrity is always redeemable for respect—a precious, highly desired commodity.

You want respect? Then demonstrate absolute truthfulness and unflinching honesty—with God, with yourself, with your spouse, and then in all the other areas of your life.

BEING DEPENDABLE

This second requirement of integrity is a real stickler in many relationships. In a broad way being dependable is connected with honesty and truthfulness; you can't be truly dependable without also being honest and truthful. But dependability is a more nitty-gritty issue. What it boils down to is responsibility. Being dependable means *assuming*, not avoiding, responsibility.

I've shared how Randy's lack of financial responsibility early in our marriage caused contention, how I worried when we couldn't make payments on time, how, when the power company threatened to cut off our electricity, I vowed to fend for myself if I couldn't depend on Randy to provide our basic needs. Nothing that ever happened in our marriage, no problems we ever faced, undermined my respect for my husband as much as his unwillingness or inability to assume financial responsibility for me and for our family.

Ours isn't the only marriage where this has happened. Not long ago I heard a far more extreme case. The husband came from a well-to-do family where everything was handed to him on a silver platter. He didn't really grow up because his parents spoiled him.

When he got married and went out on his own, the real world proved a great shock to him. He failed at a long succession of jobs, changing careers a number of times. Because of his frequent, sometimes long intervals of unemployment, his wife shouldered most of the financial load—often working two jobs to keep one step ahead of their creditors. To make matters worse, when he was fired from his most recent job, he cashed his severance check and left her at home alone to work full-time and part-time jobs *and* care for their three kids, while he went to Aspen to ski with friends. He said he "deserved a break after all he'd been through." And then he couldn't understand why she reacted so icily when he wanted to take her to bed as soon as he walked back in the door.

True story! As hard as it is to believe, this guy didn't get it. He still doesn't understand the connection between the love (even sexual attraction) his wife feels and his responsibility to provide for their family financially.

Of course, responsibility issues aren't always financial. Randy and I went through several years of parenthood with me resenting his lack of daily involvement in the care of our young children. I'd always believed since it took two people to conceive a child, God intended those same two people to care for and raise that child after he or she was born. But perhaps because of work involvement, Randy's sense of parental responsibility was often at odds with mine. Not that he neglected the kids or refused to pitch in when I'd ask. He was always a loving, affectionate father who was often ready to help. But the unspoken implication was that the primary responsibility for our children, and the greater part of their daily care, was to be mine.

The Phillips' household isn't the only place this tension has surfaced. In fact, as I've read Promise Keepers correspondence over the years, lack of responsibility in the area of parenting seems to be a frequent frustration. In fact, the second biggest need expressed by women letter writers is that their men would become better husbands and fathers by "assuming more responsibility for our kids."

Why does this seem to be such a universal complaint? Could it be because the steady degeneration of the nuclear family in recent generations has created a whole society of men without strong and consistent role models of fatherhood?

If that's true of you, you may need to do what Randy has done. Find mentors you can go to for advice, role models you can look to who can help you both see and fulfill your responsibilities of parenthood.

Would it make it any easier to know that taking part in basic child care, such as feeding, bathing, and changing young children—which so many "macho" guys evidently consider "women's work"—can actually make a guy seem even more masculine and appealing to a woman who loves him? Nothing endears Randy to me more than watching him play with or care for our children. Against the backdrop of the tender gentleness he shows our children, I see, in bold relief, the contrasting rugged strength I want and need in my leading man.

Want more respect from the woman you love? Then make sure you're assuming your share of responsibility for the love and care of your kids.

This responsibility and dependability need to carry over to other areas of your home life as well. Let's suppose you've promised your wife you'll help her this weekend do some big household project she's been itching to get to for months. Come Saturday morning you're reading the paper, and you realize you'd forgotten all about the game of the century being on TV that afternoon. So you say, "Oh, sweetheart. I've been thinking. Let's try to start that project tomorrow. Maybe right after church would be good. What do you say?"

I don't know for certain what she'll say. But I do know what she'll be thinking and feeling. That she depended on you, and you weren't dependable. That your word is not your word. That you don't have any integrity. And her respect will go right out the window. Down the drain. Up the chimney.

I've watched Randy work on all these areas of responsibility these past years. He's sought out a financial adviser to help him be more responsible with money. He regularly jumps in and helps with the kids even before I ask him. And, occasionally, he'll even come home on a Friday night after work and ask, "Holly, what do you need me to do to help you around the house this weekend?"

By consistently assuming his share of responsibility, by being dependable, Randy has increased my respect and helped transform our relationship in the process.

REMAINING FAITHFUL

Just as dependability is built on the foundation of honesty and truth, this third ingredient of integrity rests on those cornerstones *plus* dependability and responsibility. You can't "remain faithful" without demonstrating all those things we've just talked about.

An affair doesn't very often occur as a single, one-night event that just happens out of the blue. A pattern of gradual weakening always precedes it—an incremental progression of thoughts and behavior that eventually bring a person to a point where the previously "impossible and unthinkable" looks so simple, so conceivable, so realizable, that the final decision is almost inevitable. Once you get that close, your vision becomes so blurred and your thinking so fuzzy that you can no longer follow your moral compass. What you once *believed* so wrong, suddenly *feels* so right.

Some of you who have reached this point already may be wondering, *How in the world did I ever get this far?* The answer is simple. If you look back, you will almost certainly be able to distinguish the pattern in your path, a recognizable outline of your slow and steady footprints, proving the wisdom in those old Chinese proverbs: "Step by step a man goes on a long journey" and "The longest journey begins with a single step."

Those of you who determine to follow the narrow path and remain faithful may also be wondering, *How in the world do I do that?* This answer too is simple—far simpler than our permissive culture often leads us to believe. If we look ahead, we can discover for ourselves the relevant wisdom of two old American sayings: "An ounce of prevention is worth a pound of cure" and "Watch that first step; it's a doozy!"

It's those very first steps of a journey, as small and effortless and insignificant as they may seem at the time, that set our direction, establish our pattern, and thereby determine our final destination. So if you really intend to *remain* faithful to the end, you need to *be* faithful every step of the way—*especially* in those earliest, seemingly casual and inconsequential steps, which in all probability will decide the outcome of your journey.

How do you stay safely and faithfully on track in a world filled with so many traps and pitfalls?

When Randy and I lived in Hawaii we couldn't drive along Waikiki without feeling visually assaulted by the beautiful bodies, the blatant sexual behavior, and the other sexual temptations surrounding us wherever we looked. So we did what the Old Testament prophet Job did, we made a covenant (a binding and solemn agreement) with our eyes. In order to remain pure in thought and faithful to each other, we determined to look neither right nor left as we went about our business on the strip of Waikiki.

Since men are a lot more susceptible to visual temptation and stimulation than women are, I know you could benefit from the prophet's practice. Before you stroll down a crowded beach, before you walk past a newsstand full of sexually revealing magazine covers, before you stand in line at a theater box office, or sit on your sofa channel-surfing with your remote, make a covenant with your eyes. If you're more careful where you look and what you see, I guarantee you'll find it easier to stay on the path and remain faithful.

And yet making a covenant with your eyes isn't enough. You will also need to make a covenant with your feet.

Dr. Billy Graham has, on various occasions, talked about some very simple strategies he's employed over the years to avoid unnecessary temptation and remain faithful to his wife. He's carefully followed one very hard-and-fast rule he established for himself very early in his public life: He refuses to go, be, or stay anywhere private or alone with any woman other than his wife. He doesn't go out to lunch with a woman unless someone else is along. He won't ride in a car with another woman unless there are other passengers. He avoids counseling or working with a woman alone in a room. He won't even give dictation to his secretary without making sure that his office door remains open.

Sound too extreme? Consider the results. It's worked to preserve Billy Graham's integrity. How many men could have saved themselves great grief and remained faithful to their spouses if they had abided by a similar policy? Make a covenant with your feet to avoid going, being, or staying anywhere you know you will face undue temptation. Flee even the appearance of impropriety. And you too can stay on the path of faithfulness.

One other covenant will help—a covenant with your mind. Yet another well-known preacher had some wisdom that applies here. Speaking on the subject of temptation, Martin Luther once drew a rather colorful word picture. He acknowledged that "You can't keep a bird from flying over your head, but you can keep him from building a nest in your hair." In other words you can determine that when inevitable thoughts, ideas, images, and fantasies flit into your mind, you will refuse to entertain them, or allow them to dwell there until they begin to affect your behavior.

If you will make these covenants with your eyes, your feet, and your mind, you won't have to worry about your other body parts. And you'll certainly find it easier to remain faithful.

I know *making* a covenant is one thing. Keeping it is something else. So here's where phase two of our "remaining faithful" strategy comes in.

Promise Keepers makes a big deal about a man's need to be accountable—to God first, of course, to his wife naturally, but also to one or more other men who love and care about him. This accountability, which Randy didn't benefit from during the early and troubled years of our marriage, has been an invaluable asset to our relationship in recent years.

Randy and I now belong to a home group with four other couples with whom we meet once a month to fellowship, pray, and share our hearts. The guys get together for about three hours or so every other week. They help each other keep the individual covenants they've made by demanding honest answers to such questions as: *Did you see anything you shouldn't have seen this week? Did you go anywhere you had no business going? What has been occupying your mind since we got together last? Have you demonstrated honesty and truthfulness? Have you been dependable? Have you remained faithful? If not, what happened, and what do you intend to do about it?*

That Randy regularly experiences this kind of accountability makes it easier for him to be a man of integrity. His willingness to open up and make himself vulnerable by subjecting himself to the insight and authority of his Christian brothers makes me respect him all the more.

I want to make one additional point about accountability groups. They can be especially important in dealing with sexual sin—an addiction to pornography, for example. These things thrive only in the darkest, most private corners of our lives. If they are dragged out into the open of an accountability group (as hard and painful as that may seem at first), it's like turning on a light, dispelling the darkness, and removing both the place and the desire to hide. To expand the metaphor, you turn on the light and the temptations scatter like so many cockroaches. Leave the light on long enough, and those cockroaches won't come back.

So if you're serious about remaining faithful, be determined to become accountable to other men. Together you will find strategies and strength for keeping your covenants, for demonstrating honesty, being dependable, and remaining faithful. As James 5:16 advises: "Confess your sins to each other and pray for each other so that you may be healed."

You'll prove your integrity. And that, more than anything else, will earn you the respect you have always wanted.

R-E-S-P-E-C-T IS A TWO-WAY STREET

There are actually two equally viable game plans for achieving respect. So far we've talked about the first one— earning it with integrity. The second strategy involves one of those little-understood laws of the relational universe. Just as friendship begets friendship and love begets love, so too respect begets respect. Which means: *The quickest and best way to get respect is to give it.*

How do you do that?

I have a number of additional suggestions in the next chapter when we answer the question: "What Can I Do to Show Her I Really Care?" But here are a few quick thoughts to get you started—practical, powerful ways you can give respect to the woman you love.

Respecting Her Choices and Desires

This relates to the earlier question, *What does she mean when she says, "It's always been about you"?* We saw how easy and common it is for *his* concerns, interests, and needs (particularly as they relate to work) to take precedence over *hers*.

One of the most common stresses wives and mothers report today is pressure from their husbands to go back to work outside the home before they are ready to leave their children. Often this pressure is applied because the husband wants personal relief and help with the financial load or he sees something he thinks they could afford if he could count on a second paycheck. Then, not only are selfish concerns pursued at the expense of the entire family, but his wife's God-given motherly instincts and commitments have been minimized and devalued.

On the flip side, some husbands give no thought or consideration for their wives' dreams and aspirations *beyond* the home—in their careers or just their daily lives. I've told you already how devalued I felt, how devoid of personal dreams I became during those years when it seemed I was nothing more than an accessory to Randy's ministry and career. But that's changed now, as evidenced by one of the most revealing and meaningful things Randy ever did for me.

A couple of years ago, we were in the sitting area of our bedroom talking after Randy returned home from a workshop where he'd done some extensive life analysis. He'd looked back over his entire life to try to recognize and understand the patterns that had been shaping him for his life's calling. He was so excited and energized by the experience that I began to feel a little jealous.

Randy picked up on my feelings, so he pulled out a big flip chart and started giving me a summary of the seminar right there in our bedroom. "Honey," he said, "if there were five big goals, five things you wish you could do in your life, what would they be?"

With Randy standing there, his marker poised to record my answers, I tried to think. "I don't know," I told him as tears trickled down my face. "I just don't know." I was crying because I realized I'd buried my personal goals years ago.

Randy clearly didn't understand my reaction. "Maybe in terms of your music..." I tried to hold the tears back as I grieved over the personal dreams and aspirations I'd let die. In that moment, I suddenly realized this was a big part of the reason I had been living a visionless, hopeless existence for so long.

Randy continued to try to encourage me—to draw out my dreams. "Would you like to record another album?"

"Yes," I admitted. "But I don't know if I have any songs left in me."

"What else then?" Randy went on.

"I'd love to travel," I told him. "I'd love to take you to see the places in Europe where I lived as a kid."

So he wrote that down. Eventually I listed five big dreams. The last of which I told Randy, "I want to work side by side with you in your ministry. Not in different orbits. Together."

When he finished writing, Randy looked at the list for a minute and then said one of those affirming things that have affected me so deeply. "Holly," he said, "I will do whatever I can to help you realize those dreams!"

I knew he meant it. He's proved it since. And that has shown me incredible respect.

Recognize, Release, and Affirm Her God-given Potential

If this doesn't come easily and naturally, pray and ask God to show you your wife as he sees her, as he created her to be. When you begin to envision her through his eyes, you'll discover new reasons to love and appreciate her. And as you come to see and respect her for the special creation she is, it'll add a whole new dimension to your relationship. Just think—there will never be another woman to occupy time and space as your wife. Why was she created? What great things did God intend for her?

As I think of those questions, I'm reminded of yet another one of those highest of highlights from my own marriage. I will never forget the day, after God had begun tuning Randy's heart to mine, when he put his hand on me and prayed one of the most powerful prayers I've ever felt in my life: "Lord, I endorse Holly. Please release her from any restrictions or any expectations I have unfairly placed on her. I acknowledge that you have gifted her, that you've given her talents and abilities that she has yet to be allowed to exhibit in her life. So I'm asking you to do this for her— free her to be the person you intended her to be."

As Randy prayed, I felt as if a hand reached into my body to touch and correct and heal something deep in the core of my being. Afterward I told Randy, "You'll never know what that did for me for you to say that you saw how God had gifted me and wanted to use me."

But if he didn't know everything, he knew something had happened. Because he began encouraging other men to pray that same prayer.

And so do I. As a powerful means of showing respect.

Honor Her Publicly

During the 1994 Promise Keepers conference at Folsom Field in Boulder, Colorado, Randy walked out on stage to make some announcements and to introduce and thank various staff members for their work and contribution to the conference. I was proudly watching my husband from backstage, thinking he was wrapping up his comments when I heard him say:

"There's one more very special person I want you to thank today. This person worked for no pay at the very beginning of Promise Keepers—doing our correspondence and then helping create our correspondence department. I've seen this person stand behind closed doors and weep over boxes of letters we received because she was so concerned about answering them all. I'd like to introduce to you all, my best friend and roommate, my wife, Holly Phillips."

I was numb. My legs turned to rubber as I felt someone gently pushing me toward the steps onto the stage. When I crossed that platform to my grinning husband, more than fifty thousand men stood and applauded. As Randy embraced me and I began to cry, I felt one of his arms let go and reach out behind me. When I turned, he presented me with a gorgeous armload of a dozen red roses.

Wow! Talk about feeling valued! I could never have imagined anything like it.

For Randy to honor me like that gave me an unbelievable and unforgettable sense of love and respect.

Now I know not every man is in a position to laud his wife in front of an entire stadium full of clapping and cheering onlookers. But every one of you is creative enough to find a time and place (be it at church in a Sunday school class discussion, when you're out eating with friends, or maybe at some extended family gathering) to honor your wife with words of appreciation, praise, or commendation—where you could make a deliberate effort to affirm her before her peers and mentors.

Nothing would be more pleasing.

Serve Her Privately

Giving respect doesn't have to take place in public. Some ways you might do it are so personal they ought to be done in private. In fact, many of the ways Randy has demonstrated his respect for me are so personal I wouldn't feel free to discuss them here.

But what we're talking about here requires the kind of servant's attitude Paul was alluding to in that "mutual submission" passage in Ephesians. His advice in Romans 12:3, 10 seems particularly pertinent to marriage: "Do not think of yourself more highly than you ought, but rather think of yourself with sober judgment, in accordance with the measure of faith God has given you. . . . Be devoted to one another. . . . Honor one another above yourselves."

My favorite translation of this passage is where we find the phrase I used earlier, "preferring one another" in love.

That's servanthood. That's respect.

That's also the kind of example Jesus set and Paul pointed out again in Philippians 2:

> If you've gotten anything at all out of following Christ, if his love has made any difference in your life . . . if you have a heart, if you care—then do me a favor: Agree with each other, love each other, be deep-spirited friends. . . . Don't be obsessed with getting your own advantage. . . . Think of yourself the way Christ Jesus thought of himself . . . he set aside the privileges of deity and took on the status of a slave, became human! . . . he didn't claim special privileges. Instead he lived a selfless, obedient life and then died a selfless, obedient death—and the worst kind of death at that: a crucifixion. (*The Message*)

You, like Christ, can show no greater love, can pay no higher respect, than to serve.

Two stories come to mind.

The first came from Wellington Boone, one of the speakers at the 1996 Promise Keepers conference in New York City. He told about an important turning point in his life when he'd been struck with the realization of all the things his wife did to please and serve him. He was so moved by the servant example his wife had set that he vowed he was not going to let her outserve him. He set a lifelong goal of serving her by looking for ways to show his love and fulfill her needs and desires.

The first thing he did was go through her closet, pulling out any out-of-style, frumpy, or cheap (polyester) clothes and replacing them with fashionable, better quality (silk, etc.) outfits that he knew would help her feel like the beautiful woman she wanted to be. And he now regularly shops with her and for her as an expression of love and a means of serving and honoring her.

While I'd recommend you check with your wife before you clean out her closet and replace her wardrobe, you wouldn't need her prior approval to adopt the practice of one husband I heard about who served his wife by bringing her the newspaper and a cup of coffee in bed when he gently awakened her each morning. Or the man who told me he served his wife by volunteering to do the entire family's wash each week.

There are a world of possibilities for serving in every relationship, every household. Pick one.

How do I get her to respect me? How does she get you to respect her?

You both need to give God the opportunity to infuse your hearts with the attitude of a servant. When you do, you'll discover the true meaning and power of mutual submission and mutual respect. That will transform your marriage.

It has ours.

SO WHAT DOES SHE WANT FROM YOU, ANYWAY?

She wants:

- Trustworthy character deserving of respect.
- Consistent pursuit of truthfulness.
- Dependability in matters of security.
- Faithfulness to your word.
- Respect for her and others.
- You to serve her privately.
- You to introduce her to fifty thousand men and present her with a dozen red roses!

chapter 9

What Can I Do to Show Her I Really Care?

Words Plus Actions
Equal a Change in Behavior

If your heart has been changed and you now have hope, if your attitude has changed and you truly want to show and earn respect by becoming a servant leader, then this is an important question. Most men are action-oriented fixers. When guys come to me to talk about troubled marriages or to express their determination to improve their relationships, this is naturally one of the first questions they ask: What can I do to show her I really care?

It's an important question because many disheartened, skeptical women are thinking, if not saying: *Don't tell me, show me!* For so many years in so many relationships words have been spoken, and words have been spoken, and words have been spoken. But the actions haven't followed.

Sometimes actions are worth a million words. So I'm going to suggest some action points for you to consider. What follows here is not intended as a final, strict, or complete checklist where you can mark off each line, one at a time, until you're completely finished. It's more like a general, overall strategy, with a few clear objectives and a number of possible routes to achieve them. You can pick and choose and adapt the ideas that best fit you and your relationship.

Of course, by this point in the book I hope you've already picked up on some practical, winning strategies you can apply to your relationships. But I'm sure you'll consider adding some of these ideas to your "to do" list. If you try them, I think you'll find they work.

COMMUNICATE

Uh-oh! Here's that dreaded word that is often heard, but wrongfully translated, as "talk."

I immediately listed this first because I'm convinced it's so essential to any good relationship. Then I questioned whether I should even make it a separate objective at all because communication is a critical component in the other six objectives highlighted here; to achieve any of them will require meaningful, creative, perhaps even unprecedented communication. And virtually all of the strategies suggested in the remainder of this chapter involve communication.

If you're still wondering what to communicate, take another look at the cheat sheet suggested in the "What Am I Supposed to Say?" chapter. Remember those six simple words: *praise, appreciation, value,* and *needs, feelings, love* (NFL).

If you're wondering how to get started, I've got three even simpler words for you: Just do it! You'll get better with practice. And if you don't try it, you'll never know.

If you're wondering when to communicate, I've got only one word of advice: *now!*

As they say, time is of the essence. Time also seems to be one of the major obstacles to communication. So you may have to make the time.

We have friends who turn on their answering machine every night before supper and leave it on all evening. They refuse to let telephone calls interrupt their family communication time. Once they get their kids down for the night, this same couple regularly spends at least an hour alone in their hot tub communicating.

We don't all have hot tubs. Randy and I find different ways to insure our time alone to communicate. Every morning we get up early, when the kids won't interrupt. After we've read the Bible, we pray together and discuss issues we never get to talk about in the course of a day. We also go out on a "date" together at least once a week. And movies don't count—unless there's additional time to spend a good chunk of time talking over a meal or coffee later. Sometimes we'll enjoy dinner at the kind of restaurant we wouldn't take our kids to. Occasionally we'll go for a drive into the mountains or take a walk. Bike rides have always been a good way for us to spend time together. You don't need to spend any money or find some exotic setting. The point isn't *where* we communicate but that we plan a regular time to do so.

And if you're still wondering *why* you need to communicate, consider the story of a woman who wrote to Promise Keepers:

> I spent the better part of our marriage thinking up new questions to ask or trying to discover some discussion topic that would elicit more than a three-syllable response from my husband. For fifteen years all I got was the usual: "Yeah," "Uh-huh," "That's nice," "Is that right?" "I guess so," and the all-purpose "I don't know."

The day he got back from your conference he nearly talked my ear off. I couldn't get a word in edgewise for almost three straight hours. I couldn't believe it! Oh, he's still not what you'd call a big talker. But he wants to communicate with me now. He tries.

He seems like a new man to me. And we seem to have a whole new relationship. Our marriage has never been better.

LISTEN

I realize listening is actually an essential element of any effective communication. But I've made this a separate objective because it's so important to any marital game plan. I've learned its significance from personal experience and from other women—those hurting because their husbands don't *and* those who are now healing because they are.

For example, consider yet another letter written by a wife who said:

That first weekend after my husband returned from the Promise Keeper conference was difficult. On Wednesday when he opened his follow-up packet he rather hesitantly told me, "There's a place here for wives to share the difference they see in their husbands ... if they want to."

I told him, "I can write about the difference in the way you relate to our children, your employees, or our friends because I've noticed that. But I can't write about the difference in the way you relate to me, because there is no difference!" And then I cried ... as usual.

Then I saw it—the difference! He heard what I said. He asked me to explain! He was listening! He wanted me to teach him how I needed to be treated! I thought that's what I'd been trying to do for the last thirty years. But now he is really listening. Now he hears me!

He has always been a "good" man, but now he desires to be a godly man. He has always been a "good" husband, but now he desires to be a godly husband. And there is a HUGE difference.

The Lord is at work in this man of integrity, and he has given me the desire of my heart. I now feel heard, understood, and cherished by my husband, and that goes a long way toward healing the hurts of the past.

Let me tell you: It's worth the wait!

Listening makes a difference.

If you really listen, without being defensive, you may find a way out of conflict or avoid a potential conflict altogether.

If you're really and truly willing to listen and learn, you might even ask your wife the question, "What can I do to show you I really care?" or "What do I need to do to be a better husband and father?"

One guy who did this the night he got home from a Promise Keepers conference wrote to tell Randy about it:

> Lying in bed, I asked my wife, "Honey, what three things could I do to make you, the kids, and our marriage stronger, happier, more secure, and better grounded in the Lord?" Well, I knew I'd asked a huge question.
>
> The next morning I asked my wife why she hadn't answered my question. She told me that no sooner had I asked the question than I promptly fell sound asleep —snoring loudly.
>
> Fortunately my wife is a wonderful, understanding, merciful, compassionate, Proverbs 31 kind of woman—married to a man much beneath her. So she had very patiently waited till morning to give me her answer, which turned out to be a very simple and straightforward one. She told me her greatest needs would be met if I would (1) be home more, (2) do more to help around the house, and (3) laugh more when I

am home. Number three hurt me deeply, partly because it caught me by surprise, but also because it convicted me so.

I would encourage any Promise Keeper, any man, anywhere to heed the call of his family to: be available (at home); be helpful (as a servant leader); and be fun (enjoy your family). And I intend to ask my wife the same question in another six months. By then I hope she'll have three different areas of need I can meet. (I also intend to hear her answer without falling asleep.)

No telling what you'll learn if you listen.

But I do know this. If you want to go from being self-centered and thoughtless to being other-centered and thoughtful, your best and quickest way is to listen.

SHARE EACH OTHER'S WORLDS

He has his job; she has hers. She makes her circle of friends and associates; he makes his. He pursues his hobbies; she pursues hers. She takes her vacation; he takes his. He writes checks on his checking account; she writes checks on hers. She controls her side of the electric blanket; he controls his.

Is it any wonder that he has his problems and she has hers? Or that those problems so often look like "irreconcilable differences"?

There is nothing wrong with a couple developing strong self-identities as individuals. A certain amount of independence can be healthy.

But it's hard for any couple to aim for and attain the biblical model of marriage where "the two shall become one" when the *two* spend so much of their existence (both professional and personal) moving in different orbits in totally separate universes. It should come as no surprise for this couple when their close encounters make them feel more like aliens than fellow travelers, let alone partners.

What can you do to show you really care?

Look for ways to explore, observe, and share each other's worlds.

Include her in your world whenever you can. Encourage her to drop by your office or job from time to time—if only to meet you for lunch. She may need to see your work world and the people who populate it.

Few things make me feel more valued than when my husband includes me in his world this way. It's convincing evidence to me that Randy really cares whenever he invites me into his work world, even more so when he asks for my input and help.

Being together communicates volumes. Just being in the house together has made me feel a part of Randy's life. A look, a glance, a hug, a kiss during the course of a day when Randy chooses to bring his work home, makes me feel incredibly connected. Sometimes he doesn't need to talk to communicate that he cares.

You already know how incredibly meaningful it was when Randy asked me to help him by taking on the role of Promise Keeper's music liaison with the recording industry. But I haven't yet told you the story about how I came to speak to the men at PK conferences in 1995.

In 1994, when Promise Keepers was invited to make a presentation at a foundation conference for people who were looking for organizations to support financially, Randy invited me to go along with him. Since there were both men and women attending the conference, one of our staff members suggested he ask me to share in the PK presentation with him. When he broached the subject, my initial reaction was negative. I couldn't imagine what I could possibly say that would interest potential supporters. But the more Randy thought and prayed about it, the more convinced he became that I should share the platform with him. I dreaded the idea so much I actually tried to get out of going on the trip altogether at the last minute. But by the time we arrived, I'd decided what I could say: I would simply report, from one woman's up close viewpoint, what I'd seen happening with men through the Promise Keepers movement.

Still, the task ahead seemed very intimidating. The fifteen-minute time slot we were assigned fell smack-dab between two Chucks—Swindoll and Colson. I thought, *How in the world do we speak between men like them?* But when I walked up to the podium in that elegant hotel ballroom and looked out at all those folks, God calmed my racing heart and steadied me as for six or seven minutes I simply talked and shared my heart. I couldn't help getting a little choked up as I recounted my emotional reaction at the first conference of 4,200 men—how I, as a woman, had felt so moved by the power and potential I saw in that multitude of committed men. But I made it through my part of our presentation.

What truly affirmed and almost overwhelmed me was the response we had afterwards. What a boost for my confidence level to have men I respected so much—like Chuck Swindoll from Insight for Living and Chuck Colson from Prison Fellowship, James Dobson from Focus on the Family, and Bruce Wilkinson from Walk Through the Bible— make a special point of commending me there in front of my husband. But what was every bit as meaningful were the responses of the men in the audience; so many of them thanked me for sharing and helping their wives see the validity and the promise of Promise Keeper's ministry.

Randy, in hearing all these responses, suddenly saw the simple, but persuasive power of a woman's perspective on Promise Keepers. By the time we walked out of that ballroom, he was thinking. Before we even got back to our hotel room, he asked, "Holly, how would you feel about speaking to the men at one of the conferences this year?"

"Well," I told him, "it would be an awesome privilege!"

I celebrated my fortieth birthday that weekend. And it was like a coming-out party for me. I felt so loved, so appreciated, and blessed that Randy believed in me, knew God had used me, and would even consider involving me in his ministry in such a way.

When we got home Randy proposed the idea at his next staff meeting. And the rest (as they say) is history. Instead of speaking at one conference, I had the privilege of speaking at all of them—eleven in person, two via videotape.

Now I realize not every man is in a position to ask his wife to publicly, or even privately, represent him and his company. Not many men even have a platform they can offer to share. But undoubtedly there are other ways you can include your wife in your world of work or ministry.

If you have a problem or a decision you're wrestling with on the job, discuss it with her. Invite her opinion. Brainstorm possibilities together. Ask her to help you think through and list the pros and the cons. You show that you really care whenever you find ways to help her personally connect with that very big part of your life.

But it's not enough just to give her points of entrance to your world. You can also venture into hers—to see her living and breathing in her own atmosphere, her own environment—whether that's at home or away.

Stop by her work to take her to lunch. Know her colleagues—have faces to put with the names you hear at home and with the voices on the phone. Attend her office Christmas (and other) parties.

If she engages in hobbies or other interests, you can show you care by learning something about them. You needn't take up needlepoint, but care enough to know what project she's working on and notice the progress she's made. You don't have to join her when she enrolls in an aerobics program (even if you could use the exercise), but you could always encourage her by telling her how proud you are of her efforts.

You might venture into her home world through a variety of doors. Next time one of the kids is sick and out of school, you might offer to be the one to miss work and stay home. Or volunteer to take charge of the kids and the household—for an evening, a day, a weekend, or however long you think you can last—so that she can do something she needs to do for herself. As thousands of men (most of whom had to be forced into Mr. Mom roles) can testify, those experiences of trying to perform your wife's every-day roles can give you valuable insight into her world and into her.

But whatever ways you find to venture into your wife's world will make it that much easier to achieve the following objectives.

RECOGNIZE AND APPRECIATE HER

Remember what we said in chapter 4 about valuing your wife not only for what she does, but for who she is? Two quick stories where Randy did both.

Some years ago I checked into the hospital for tests. My doctor kept me hospitalized for several days of treatment and concluded my symptoms had been prompted by acute stress and exacerbated by the daily pressures of my personal and professional life. He was probably right because, when it came time to check out of the hospital, I didn't want to go home. I didn't want to walk back into my home and face the "to do" list I knew would be waiting for me.

Sensing my feelings, Randy did something very special and affirming when we got home. He gathered our three kids together and walked them through every single room of our house, starting on the second floor and working his way down to the ground floor and finally into the basement. In every room he stopped and pointed out to our kids everything I did that ultimately makes their lives easier.

In the bedrooms: "See that closet full of clothes? Your mom bought you those clothes. She ironed that dress and hung it there. See that bed? She puts fresh sheets on it. See that floor? She vacuums that. See that wallpaper border? She not only searched all over town to find that wallpaper border you like so much, she put it up."

On and on Randy went. Everywhere he looked, in every room he found more to point out.

In the kitchen: "See that food in the pantry? Your mother spends hours every week buying groceries and keeping that stocked. See that stove? Think about how many meals your mother has cooked for us. See those pots and pans, those dishes? How many times do you think she's washed those? Look at that calendar. Count the number of activities your mom drives you to each week."

In the basement: "Look at that mountain of wash. Thirteen loads a week your mother does!"

By the time he finished I should have been exhausted at the very thought of it all. Instead, I was heartened when he concluded his lecture saying, "We've been taking your mother for granted around here. And I don't ever want it to happen again. From now on we're not only going to try to appreciate everything she does for us, we're going to do a lot better job of helping out and easing her load!"

In recognizing and appreciating what I do Randy was showing me he really cared, and that he'd been noticing.

Story number two will always be just as memorable:

Randy has always been creative in his gestures of love. The traditional dozen roses isn't his usual style. So I was pleased, but not overly surprised one afternoon, when Randy came home and presented me with an arrangement of dried Colorado wildflowers. What made that day so memorable—what moves me so every time he's brought me wildflowers since—were his words as he handed me that bouquet. He explained that the wildflowers reminded him of me, that "You are my bouquet of wildflowers. Bright and bursting with color, full of variety, everblooming ..."

None of the things he said, none of the comparisons he made, described what I "do." He was demonstrating his love by noticing who I "am." Which showed me just how much he cares.

If you're thinking, *I'm not that creative with words. I don't think I could ever do that!* I've got a suggestion for you. Pick up a copy of *The Blessing* by John Trent and Gary Smalley. They spell out a step-by-step process for using words that bless your loved ones by recognizing and appreciating them both for who they are and who God wants them to be.

BE HER BOOSTER CLUB

A lot of parents are very familiar with this concept. If you don't have kids in school yet, think back on your own growing up days. Most high schools have athletic boosters, and band boosters, sometimes even academic booster clubs. Since you probably know what booster clubs do, you can probably already anticipate some of what I mean when I say "Be her booster club." I mean:

You could plan on being there for her—through thick and thin, good and bad times. *Celebrate her successes to be sure. But also pick her up and hug her when she loses.*

Encourage her to "go for it." Following are some examples of what I'm talking about—when Randy did this for me, when he has urged me to aim higher, to get out of my rut, to stretch myself.

Some time ago now I heard about a course being offered in the traditional German practice of *scherenschnitte*, the delicate art of cutting small, intricate designs in folded paper with tiny scissors. When I absentmindedly mentioned that "I'd love to take that class," Randy responded. "Why not? It's only $25. We can afford it. Call and register now." So I did, though I never would have pursued it without Randy's encouragement. I had a blast.

Another time Randy spotted a notice in the Denver paper announcing auditions for the Colorado Symphony Choir. This was during a time when I was not provided the opportunity to use my musical skills through the church where we attended. "You ought to go down and audition," he said.

"I don't think so. What chance would I have?" I responded.

"I bet you could make it," he prodded. "What can it hurt? Give it a try. Nothing ventured, nothing gained."

I agreed—reluctantly. I rehearsed a piece of music for two weeks. Then when it came time, I remember Randy went with me to the tryouts. I also remember him pushing our infant daughter in her stroller along the downtown sidewalks of Denver to the Concert Center. I remember him holding me after I came out of the vocal trial room—trembling with emotion.

I also remember how I whooped and hollered and danced through the house when I got the word that I made it. Randy brought all the kids to the concerts to hear me sing. And what I'll never forget about the whole experience is how Randy believed in me, how he saw potential and possibilities even when I didn't.

He's always showing how much he cares by encouraging me to step out on my own. Sometimes it's a small step: "Why don't you go see that movie?"

"By myself?"

"Why not? I know you'd like it, and I'm not really interested. So go!"

Other times the stakes seem a lot bigger: "Write a book? I don't know," I said.

"You've got something important to say! Do it!"

Sometimes Randy goes beyond encouragement to challenge—like when he says, "I think you should do it, Holly, or you're not using all the potential God has given you." And sometimes I need that.

But I would warn you to be gentle with your challenges.

Most women already feel incredible pressure to perform. They don't need another coach nearly as much as they need you to be a cheerleader and their biggest booster.

Oh, and just as a sidenote—when it comes to the relationship between your kids and your spouse—please don't let your kids abuse her with words or disrespectful behavior. She would cherish your coming to her defense and being her knight in shining armor. She is your beloved. Would you let anyone else talk to her that way? Why would you let your kids?

TAKE LEADERSHIP

The most common desire expressed by women writing to Promise Keepers is this: They long for their husbands to take spiritual leadership in their family.

We aren't wanting our husband to do all the praying or to serve as some superspiritual authority, constantly preaching at the family, or quoting Bible verses for every occasion. But some of the time you might be the one to suggest, "We need to pray about that." You don't need to preach or make big moral pronouncements; you can be spiritual leaders simply by sharing from time to time what new spiritual insights you are learning in your own lives. You don't need to be a Bible scholar, but we'd be glad for you to point out a truth when you see how God's Word applies. We'd be thrilled if you would exhibit your leadership by making your own and the family's spiritual needs a priority. We'd be relieved if it weren't left to us to address the spiritual needs in the home.

Here's one letter from a woman reporting on her husband's new spiritual leadership:

> Our lives have not been the same. Five out of seven mornings he wakes me at 5 A.M. to pray with him. The other two mornings he goes to his Promise Keepers group. Sometimes when we are praying I have to open my eyes just to be sure this is the same man I've been married to for eighteen years. Our relationship is being restored and changed every day. After not receiving much attention and/or care for several years, it is sometimes overwhelming to be on the other end of so much love. He has truly turned one hundred percent of his life over to God. Today he was baptized at church—something I've prayed about for years.
>
> But the most precious change for me to see has been seeing him turn toward our children. I sometimes catch our youngest son looking at him with an expression that says, "Where did you come from?" They are spending so much more time together and working on their communication skills.
>
> My husband is a changed man.

This woman's letter, and many more, indicate that real leadership needs to include spiritual leadership.

What else is real leadership?

Real leadership is knowing how and when to take charge and use your strengths. But it's also being mature enough to know and admit your weaknesses. And being confident enough in your masculinity to follow her lead where she is strong.

There's a difference between leadership and dictatorship. And Jesus' servant-leadership model will keep you from confusing the two.

BECOME AN INITIATOR

You could pretty much sum up all the suggestions in this chapter in this final objective. But I first saw this in

Randy and understood its application to our relationship in those months after the Lord began to change him back in 1990. For the first time, Randy initiated discussion, acknowledged any offenses where he had been neglectful, sought my forgiveness, and made deliberate and positive changes in our relationship. Each time he assumed the role of initiator in some way, it was as if he was pouring a bucket of cool, soothing water on my fire.

For so long before, whenever he seemed inconsiderate or just neglectful, I was like a drought-stricken forest ignited with a match. I'd become an all-consuming fire jumping from tree to tree, from issue to issue, seeking fuel for retaliation in reaction to Randy's lack of initiation. Through much of our life together, most of Randy's and my relationship was shaped and colored by our *reaction* to each other.

If you look up the word *reaction* in the dictionary you find it's a "contrary or opposing action." That was me. That was us. My heart was definitely in opposition to my husband's. And I was certainly "contrary."

It wasn't until he became an initiator that I began to respond instead of react. *To respond* means "to reply: answer. *To react* positively."

Returning to our imagery of putting out a fire, I see myself more as a forest *after* a devastating blaze. Because my husband faithfully and consistently initiated change one bucketful at a time, the fire was doused. The forest is responding and recovering—manifesting all sorts of new growth.

My heart has been slowly softened and warmed as Randy has initiated love and care for me. I've been falling in love with him again ever since. I'm responding with tenderness and thankfulness now instead of reacting with hatred or disgust—or even worse, complete indifference.

One day, as we both master the meaning of "preferring one another" in love, we'll learn that we each can be the initiator. In our case, Randy initiated and I responded. Only slowly, through Randy's example as a servant leader showing in so many ways that he really cares, am I learning to become an initiator myself—instead of always expecting him to initiate.

Bless Randy and my Lord Jesus for their patience with me.

Finally, let me add this word of encouragement to any guys asking, "What can I do to show her I really care?"

Please realize that resolving the problems in your relationship isn't all your responsibility. Your wife shares responsibility. And you can't force her to accept responsibility any more than you can force her to change.

But if you want to show her you really care, you can begin by allowing yourself to be changed—your heart, attitude, and behavior. If you can be the initiator—sharing each other's worlds, offering positive affirmation, providing a chance to talk, listening, cheerleading, providing spiritual leadership, and praying against the enemy who is out to sabotage your intimacy—your wife will notice, and chances are your relationship will be transformed.

Maybe, just maybe, your wife will say something like the woman who wrote my husband to say:

Dear Randy,
What did you do with my husband?

He went to a Promise Keepers conference and never came back. There's a guy who looks a lot like him, who showed up and lives here now. But it's obviously not the same guy.

Because this man asks what I think and listens to my response. This man is involved in the lives of our children. This man is praying for me.

The man who left here to go to the conference was, frankly, a frog. This guy who came back is a prince. I don't know what you did with my husband, but you can keep him.

I'll take this guy instead.

SO WHAT DOES SHE WANT FROM YOU, ANYWAY?

She wants you to:

- Communicate.
- Listen.
- Share each other's worlds.
- Recognize and appreciate her.
- Be her booster club.
- Take leadership.
- Become an initiator.

chapter **10**

What Does She *Need* from Me, Anyway?

We titled this book with a question because so many guys are asking, *What does she want from me, anyway?* This umbrella of a question, once opened up, covers a lot of territory for many different men. At the same time it's a very personal question—an honest, heartfelt query revealing an edge of frustration.

What does she want from me, anyway? is a loaded question. I appreciate and respect you guys who have the courage to ask. And I know we've spent a whole book now trying to answer you. But I've come to the conclusion that what is the *right* title for this book may be the *wrong* question to ask.

Think about the word *want. Want* means to desire—wish for, fancy, covet, expect, maybe even demand—something. In contrast, *need* means to crave—to require, to yearn, long, or hunger for, to thirst after—something.

Our *wants* can be fickle; they may vary from person to person, even day to day. Our *needs* are constants; we all have them. Sometimes *wants* may be insignificant, even trivial. But our *needs* are fundamental requirements.

Most of us learn early in life that we can't have everything we *want*. Most of us are also taught that every human being has certain basic needs he (or she) deserves to have met. Because *wants* and *needs* may sometimes overlap, we often confuse them in our own minds. But at some level we know they are distinctly different.

So suppose you alter the question. Instead of "What does she *want* from me, anyway?" you ask, "What does she *need* from me, anyway?" Feel the greater sense of seriousness, of urgency? It's a lot harder to shrug off or ignore *needs*, as opposed to *wants*.

Now approach the revised question from a different direction. Turn it around and ask it not about her, but about yourself. What do *you* need from her, anyway? How do *you* want to be treated?

After living with Randy for twenty-three years, I've discovered a number of things men *need*.

A man needs:

- Respect—This is Randy's number-one need. Everything else takes a distant backseat.
- To be honored in his own home—I figure that's more than reasonable considering how much he does that directly benefits the family.
- To be desired sexually and emotionally—I was surprised that this was such a biggie. It was difficult for Randy to admit because it made him vulnerable. For me to learn this about him, he had to humble himself and acknowledge that a part of him was "in need." It made me sad to realize he had to do that—

that I'd been so consumed by my needs that I was oblivious to this one of his.

- To be needed. (And wanted.)
- To be considered the "most" important person in his wife's universe.
- To be cheered on in his interests.
- To be understood as "not perfect" but as a human being who bruises, who has fears and tears and weaknesses.
- To be allowed mistakes. (Too often, we women are short on mercy.)
- A *wife*—not a *mother.* (I must constantly remind myself of this, so I don't emasculate him with my *mothering.*)
- A partner who is proud to bear his children.
- A woman who is strong and confident enough in herself that she is not too threatened to allow him to lead.

So what do you think? How true is this "needs" list for you?

Now against that backdrop of your needs, you might want to reconsider the question, "What does she *need* from me, anyway?"

We've already talked about some of the most common needs expressed by women writing to Promise Keepers. Here they are along with a few more I've added from my own personal experience, from observation, and from the testimony of other women.

A woman needs:

- A husband willing to assume spiritual leadership of the family.
- A partner in parenting, not just in the baby-making.
- A husband who will care about the things that matter to her and provide her the opportunity to pursue her desires, hopes, dreams.

- For her man not to love his work so much that she has to compete with it. (In other words, she needs him to love her and find more of his fulfillment in her, their marriage, and their family.)
- To be listened to.
- To be considered.
- To feel secure.
- To be valued for who she is, not just what she does for everyone.
- To be respected and taken seriously.
- To be appreciated—not taken for granted.
- A valiant defender, a knight in shining armor, not a fief lord.
- A real man who will take the most difficult role there is—leader—and do it justice. (He needs to be strong enough to take charge, but wise enough to see and acknowledge her abilities, knowledge, and insights and to follow her lead when it's obvious she is the one who has what is needed.)

See any similarities in what you need and what she needs? You should. Because in truth, her needs are your needs and your needs are her needs.

A word of caution here: I feel compelled to say that no one person can, or was meant to, meet all of our needs. We can each benefit from a broader support system. And even then we'll have some needs only a personal relationship with God can fulfill.

But that only reinforces the perspective God had when he created the high and holy sacrament of marriage with the idea that "the two shall become one." If or when you embrace this biblical ideal, you'll gain a fresh perspective on your relationship. Then you will be able to achieve a marriage that meets both of your needs.

part **3**

Final Words

chapter *11*

Men and Women at Work

We would have been shortsighted if this book ended without at least acknowledging the fact that not all men are married, and that not all your relationships with women are romantic or even familial. You also work with women.

While I've been writing almost exclusively about marriage relationships—to men and on behalf of women who are married—I realize some very different dynamics come into play when men and women interact on a job. Yet many of the principles and ideas we've covered could apply there as well.

I'm well aware, through personal work experience and additional exposure to a variety of companies and organizations, that career women (some of whom are single) are also toting around a heavy load of significant, often very justified anger.

For example, a woman who works in a male-majority environment may experience discrimination. She may be the object of unfair salary discrepancies. She may be doing the brunt of the work or outperforming a male colleague only to see him honored with perks, raises, or public recognition. As she watches him celebrate a promotion, she learns to quit hoping for one, because a woman has never been promoted in her company. In many workplaces, the bias isn't even intentional—it's simply the way it's always been. As a result, many women have experienced some of the same kind of discrimination ethnic minorities have had to endure.

Please don't get too defensive about what I'm saying. I'm not speaking out of bitterness. I've not been biding my time, waiting impatiently for this opportunity to finally launch into a male-bashing, faultfinding tirade. That's not what this is. But some hard truths do need to be honestly recognized and addressed.

First, I want to say something on behalf of the majority of the women you work with. I am one of these women. So I know their hearts when I say, we don't want to compete with you, take your job, or usurp your authority. We would just like to work *with* you. We would like to have equal opportunity for advancement, to receive the same wages when we have the same job or workload.

Most of us haven't made it our prime objective either to invade your space or replace you. But an increasing number of us, just like people of color, are weary of being placated and patronized. All we're looking for is equal (not special) consideration.

So I want to appeal to your sense of fairness. I know that many of you are not directly involved in the pay and "placing" of women within your organization. Yet every one of you is in a position where you can give honor and respect where honor and respect are due.

As you become more understanding and aware of your wife's needs, I would hope that same kind of sensitivity would carry over to those interactions you have with women on the job. If you see or know of any person, man or woman, not being duly honored for her work, her integrity, her leadership, isn't it "right" that you speak up for her? It may not be personally expedient, but certainly right. Right?

Most men want women to be fairly treated in the workplace. Indeed, the majority of men I've known and interacted with in my various jobs didn't have an attitude or a bias against me or other female coworkers. And yet, even among the most sensitive and enlightened men, I've often noticed a lack of awareness about the inequities women have to deal with regularly.

Ask yourself:

How many women are in managerial leadership in your business? How many women serve on the board of your organization? How many management and executive decisions affecting many females are made in your company without any woman being provided the opportunity to give input or represent the needs of women employees?

The business world might benefit from more of the input provided recently by a working woman I know of who was given opportunity to address her male bosses and coworkers:

"Your wives at home should be honored. But at work, what we women would really appreciate is respect!" What she, in fact, meant was: Flowers are nice. And standing up and giving us public recognition for a job well done during the annual Christmas Gala is thoughtful. But what we'd truly appreciate is more daily respect for our input, our ideas, and our contribution. To respect us would mean understanding we too have plans and responsibilities outside the office—not unlike those of our bosses and fellow workers. When last-minute assignments demanding "urgent" and "immediate" attention are dropped on our desks at the very end of the day, we take them seriously. But are we expected to set aside our personal plans? Would you be willing to do the same?

The Golden Rule—do unto others as you would have them do unto you—applies equally well in marriage and workplace relationships. Many working women would ask of male superiors, colleagues, and subordinates: "Would you please consider how you want to be treated, and extend that same regard to us?"

As a positive example I want to share an incredibly redeeming example of growing awareness and fairness in the workplace.

Some time ago, in a discussion about who should attend an upcoming Promise Keepers managerial retreat, Randy asked his senior management team to come up with a list of all managers in the organization who were currently overseeing twenty or more employees. The research showed, much to everyone's surprise, that seven out of eight such managers in the national office were female. The first decision made as a result of that "discovery" was to invite all seven women managers on the management retreat. Then the team decided to check and make sure these women were all receiving wages commensurate with their managerial responsibilities. Promise Keepers is determined to be fair with women—as with people of color—and to make sure that the organization is honoring all God's children as he sees them—as equals.

I don't think much more needs to be said on this subject. I would simply ask you to remember the perspective of the Lord who created us all—male and female. The Bible tells us he sees "neither Jew nor Greek, slave nor free, male nor female" (Galatians 3:28). He, our Father and

Maker, doesn't play favorites (Acts 10:34). To him we are all equal and the same.

If that's true, how can it be right to stand by (knowingly) and see any coworker being used or abused—whether verbally or otherwise—on the job, and not speak up or take action on their behalf? Whether they are male or female?

Basic fairness. Equal treatment and consideration. That is all most women want and need in the workplace. Would you, as a man, settle for anything less?

chapter 12

Holly and Randy Sign Off

HOLLY

I've had my say for more than two hundred pages now. So you may be glad to know I don't have much to add. I've run my lap of the race, and I'm about to hand the baton to you. As you go farther and deeper in your relationship, I'd recommend that you get more insight and strength from additional resources that I'll suggest at the very end of the book. But before I let go of the baton completely, I want to say this:

I had a sense of urgency to communicate with you via a book that you could get your hands on, a book that was not slamming you or assaulting your manhood or degrading your place on earth. So . . . if you read this book to its final conclusion; if there was no question in your heart that you were being respected as a man in the tone that I took;

if you feel as though you may finally understand and have a handle on the answers to the questions you may have been asking for years; if you don't feel you were backed into a corner and scolded with a finger in your face; if after reading this book, you have been filled with hope for the future and have been challenged to find ways to honor and prefer your wife—then my heart's goal for writing this book is realized.

I did not write this book to tickle ears, nor to be politically correct. I was interested in only one thing, and that was to speak the truth in love. I've heard it said, "Truth without love is brutality, love without truth is hypocrisy."

As long as I have been a believer, I have found that the Bible and the character of God have integrity. And that has never wavered! The Bible has challenged me over and over again, and when I have chosen to embrace its counsel—without fail—I have always reaped a great benefit. In confronting the character, integrity, and love of God, I have never been sorry, only deeply and profoundly grateful.

I knew this book and its conclusions were not going to be palatable to everyone. I was fully prepared for that at the onset. But I will say this—everything I've said has been tested against the best elements I know: truth, time, and God's unending love. If you ever need God, his counsel, or his hope, he is only a request away ... because of Jesus of Nazareth.

Finally, I've heard some women say that "You can't talk to men." "They don't have ears to hear." "They only care about themselves." "It's a man's world, and we have no voice or place in it, except to have their babies and wait on them hand and foot." But do you know what? In these last six years, while interacting with men from all over our nation, I've found you to be hungry for the truth, wanting help, desirous for change—and it's the rare bird who felt he was "above it all."

When some people learned what I was writing about, they expressed serious doubts. "You think you'll get men to read a book about relationships? A magazine article maybe—if their wives hand it to them. But a book?"

So to those of you who have stuck with me all the way to the end—thank you. I'm gratified, but not really surprised. I knew we could talk!

RANDY

I see more than a little irony in the fact that Holly actually finished this book and asked me to share my reactions to the manuscript while in Hawaii for a Promise Keepers conference. We were together again in Honolulu—where we first met, dated, and married twenty-four years ago, where our first son was born and our second was conceived, where we received our start in ministry and began the journey that has shaped us into the individuals and the couple we are today.

Everywhere I turn on this island there are memories. Some as welcome and pleasurable as the fragrance of a tropical flower lei. Others as regrettable and painful as an unexpected encounter with a coral reef. In much the same way, every page I turn in this book, every chapter I read, brings more memories, both bitter and sweet.

Another parallel came to me:

Yesterday, here in this tropical paradise, a friend from the mainland who knew I'd lived in the islands for seven years asked if I'd ever taken the spectacular beauty of Hawaii for granted. "I guess I did," I admitted, thinking back on those days when I had allowed the new and exciting challenges of work and the unrelenting routine of daily life to so absorb my energies that I had little left with which to enjoy living here. My mind had become so preoccupied with the demands and details of life that I couldn't appreciate, and hardly even noticed, the beauty surrounding me.

Reading the manuscript of this book, it hit me: for years I did the same thing in my marriage. I was attracted to Holly because I saw beauty in her: She had (and still has) the most exuberant love for life of anyone I've ever met. Her spirit was so contagious that my heart was drawn to hers like a magnet. And I fell deeply in love.

However, as the years went by—as the demands of life, the workplace, and children mounted—I lost sight of the incredible beauty I had first seen in Holly. What's worse, by taking her for granted, I came perilously close to destroying the beauty and the spirit that made her so special to begin with.

Some of you may be wondering how I feel about all that Holly has included in this book. Obviously she has shared many intimate—some shameful, some wonderful—things we've been through in our relationship. And I admit to having some mixed feelings as I read them here in black and white.

I don't really mind being "transparent." I've learned among Christians a certain amount of "aw-shucks, I'm not so perfect" transparency is not only accepted, it's almost expected. In fact, you can gain a measure of respect when using careful doses of transparency. So the transparency here is not really that difficult to take.

It's vulnerability that scares me to death. Being truly vulnerable requires honestly sharing enough of yourself that you run the risk of being misunderstood, of being judged. And none of us enjoys feeling that exposed.

The temptation even for Christians is to try to put a happy face on everything. We can be transparent enough to admit past mistakes, but not really vulnerable enough to expose the weaknesses and the sinful nature we're wrestling with every day. And yet this inclination to put on a false front, this desire to look good or at least better than we are, can result in hypocrisy. So as uncomfortable as I get in the arena of self-disclosure, I have to thank God for Holly's honesty—which is another one of those traits that attracted me to her and which I now appreciate more than ever before. Together we pray that God will use her honesty and vulnerability to prevent others from making the same mistakes we did.

Recently I came across a quotation that seems to apply to what you and I have been reading here:

> The individual parts of a ship, taken by themselves, would sink. If you tried to set an engine on the water, it would immediately sink to the ocean bottom. A propeller would sink. So would any of the other thousands of pieces that make up a ship. Even piled together they form nothing more than an incongruent heap. But when those same parts of a ship are properly assembled, when they are built together, they float.

So it has been with the events of our lives. Some have been tragic. Some have been wonderful. But together they form a craft that not only floats but is actually going someplace. And that encourages me.

When I read those words, I immediately thought of my marriage. There were so many occasions when it seemed one of the individual "parts" we were wrestling with at the time would sink and drown us. The pieces of our lives—the choices, the feelings, the distance that grew between us—brought us to the very brink of disaster.

Only when we completely handed over our lives—the entire heap of individual pieces—into the hands of the Master builder did we begin to see something wonderful take shape. The Lord took even the broken pieces—our worst decisions and our greatest weaknesses—and made our marriage into a vessel that not only floats and is going somewhere, but a vessel fit for his use in carrying this message of hope to others in shipwrecked relationships.

I happened across another thought-provoking quote recently:

> Most men fail not because they are stupid, but because they are not sufficiently impassioned.

That was certainly true of me and my marriage. For too many years I was not impassioned. Why not? What happened?

We're not impassioned because we don't have a proper vision. We lose our passion in marriage because we fail to see our marriage or our wives as the Lord sees them. When we don't have a clear picture of what God has in mind for the future of our marriages, we involve ourselves in lesser things. We lose the discipline and the commitment needed to invest the love, the communication, the respect, the appreciation, the support, and the sacrificial service required to build the strong and stable relationship God designed marriage to be.

How do we find (or regain) that vision? As you finish reading this book there may be no better time for you to take the opportunity to step back and honestly examine the bitter and the sweet memories of your own marriage, to yield all the pieces of your life and relationships into the Master builder's hand—to do what only he can. You might pray something like this:

"God, let me see my wife as you see her. Lord, let me see those things in my life that are not yielded to you and are not demonstrating the love you want me to have for her. God, show me those things I can do that are like you—as you loved us as your church and gave yourself for us. Let me reflect that kind of sacrificial love. Please give me the strength daily to see and do those little things I can do and you might use, to enable my wife to blossom and grow in ways she has never experienced or imagined."

If we as men pray that prayer, not just once and for all time, but as often as possible, I believe God will share his vision for our marriage, and give us the passion we need to succeed—to provide all that our spouses want and need from us and our relationship.

We definitely can't do it ourselves. Not in our own power. Experience should have proved that by now—even for those of us who are slow learners. But I love what the apostle Paul says in this one final quote from Galations 5:

> When you attempt to live by your own religious plans and projects, you are cut off from Christ. ... For in Christ, neither our most conscientious religion, nor disregard for religion, amounts to anything. What matters is something far more interior. Faith expressed in love....
>
> For everything we know about God's word is summed up in a single sentence: *Love others as you love yourself* (THE MESSAGE).

BOOKS AND RESOURCE LIST

If you've finished this book and are ready to continue the race, here are some resources I recommend. No matter how far you've come in your own life or marriage, you'll find help here that will carry you farther and deeper in your relationships.

To help on your spiritual journey
Experiencing God by Henry Blackaby and Claude King
The Jesus I Never Knew by Philip Yancey
The Root of the Righteous by A.W. Tozer
Keys to the Deeper Life by A.W. Tozer
What God Does When Men Pray by William Carr Peel

On the topic of you and your manhood
Tender Warrior by Stu Webber
Real Men Have Feelings Too by Gary Oliver
Straight Talk to Men by James Dobson
Guard Your Heart by Gary Rosberg
Brothers! Calling Men into Vital Relationships
    by Geoff Gorsuch and Dan Schaffer
Iron Sharpens Iron by Howard Hendricks
Locking Arms by Stu Webber
Point Man by Steve Farrar
Real Men by Edwin Louis Cole

Regarding your relationship with your wife
Making Love Last Forever by Gary Smalley
Strategies for a Successful Marriage by E. Glenn Wagner
119 Ways to Love Your Wife by Gary Smalley

For you as a parent
The Blessing by John Trent and Gary Smalley
Key to a Child's Heart by Gary Smalley
The Seven Secrets of Effective Fathers by Ken R. Canfield
Tough Love by James Dobson
How to Really Love Your Child by Ross Campbell
Dear Dad by Doug Webster
Standing Tall by Steve Farrar
Homes of Honor a video series with Gary Smalley

On the topic of sex
Intended for Pleasure by Ed and Gaye Wheat
The Act of Marriage by Tim and Beverly LaHaye
Men and Sex by Cliff and Joyce Penner
Sexual Man by Archibald Hart

Addressing the issue of sexual abuse
The Wounded Heart by Dan P. Allender
Hiding from Love by John Townsend
When Victims Marry by Don and Jan Frank
Your Wife Was Sexually Abused by John Courtright
    and Sid Rogers

For the area of finances
Master Your Money by Ron Blue
Storm Shelter by Ron Blue

We want to hear from you. Please send your comments about this book
to us in care of the address below. Thank you.

ZondervanPublishingHouse
Grand Rapids, Michigan 49530
http://www.zondervan.com